The Lincolnshire Village Book

Compiled by the Lincolnshire
Federations of Women's Institutes from notes
and illustrations sent by Institutes in the County

Published jointly by
Countryside Books, Newbury
and
the LNFWI, Louth
the LSFWI, Sleaford

First Published 1990
© Lincolnshire Federations of Women's Institutes 1990

Countryside Books
3 Catherine Road
Newbury, Berkshire

ISBN 1 85306 077 1

Cover Photograph of Fiskerton
taken by Sylvia Newby

Produced through MRM Associates, Reading
Typeset by Microset Graphics Ltd., Basingstoke
Printed in England by J.W. Arrowsmith Ltd., Bristol

The
Lincolnshire
Village Book

THE VILLAGES OF BRITAIN SERIES

Other counties in this series include:

Avon*
Bedfordshire*
Berkshire*
Buckinghamshire*
Cambridgeshire*
Cheshire*
Devon*
Dorset
Essex*
Gloucestershire*
Hampshire
Herefordshire*
Hertfordshire*
Kent
Lancashire*
Leicestershire* & Rutland*

Middlesex*
Northamptonshire*
Nottinghamshire*
Oxfordshire
Powys Montgomery*
Shropshire*
Somerset*
Staffordshire*
Suffolk
Surrey
East Sussex
West Sussex
Warwickshire*
West Midlands*
Wiltshire
Worcestershire*

*Published in conjunction with the County Federation of
Women's Institutes

Foreword

Lincolnshire has always been renowned as the premier agricultural County. It lies to the east of the main north-south routes, and has the largest stretch of coastline in eastern England, popular during the summer months with visitors mainly from the midlands.

A County of contrasts, the rich fertile fenland in the south is well known for its production of tulip bulbs, brassicas and soft fruit. The central area has leafy lanes with vast acres of cereal crops, and in the north are the rolling wooded slopes of the Lincolnshire Wolds.

Over the last few years, with the popularity of the Spalding Flower Festival, the beauty of Lincoln Cathedral and with more leisure time available, people have discovered the County.

This book is intended to give some idea of the interesting villages and buildings in the area, and to quell the myth that the whole of the County is flat!

Betty Dudman
Pam Jackson
County Chairmen

Acknowledgements

The Lincolnshire Federations of Women's Institutes wish to thank all the members who have submitted contributions for this book, with special thanks for the co-ordinators of this project, Molly Andrew and Liz Sordy.

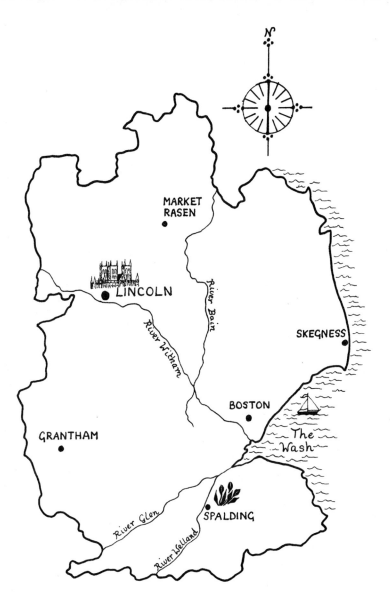

County of
LINCOLNSHIRE

Aby

A small village of less than 200 inhabitants, Aby bears the dual distinction of having the shortest place name in Lincolnshire and of occupying first place in any alphabetical listing for the county. The name of 'Aby' has its origins in the Old Norse word signifying water – 'Aby' is 'village by the water'. The water in question is that of the river Great Eau which flows through the village, providing the basis for a flourishing trout farm and the source of much good fishing. Footpaths following part of its course allow public enjoyment of this crystal clear water, its beauty enhanced by the presence of herons, geese, swans, a variety of ducks and the occasional kingfisher.

Aby (or Abi) was mentioned in the Domesday Book, its lands then being owned by Odo (Bishop of Bayeux and half brother of William the Conqueror) and Earl Hugh (Hugh the Wolf). At this time 27 acres of woodland were available for pannage (feeding swine) and it is interesting to note that at the edge of Aby there still exists 'Swinn Wood', the name also of a row of houses in the village.

Aby has an attractive location at the foot of the Lincolnshire Wolds and is formed almost in a square with a central playing field, the majority of housing being obscured from the view of travellers on the main road through the village. Herbert Green in his *Village Life* descriptions written at the turn of the century called the area 'one of the prettiest parts of Lincolnshire' and made reference to the attractive gardens bordering the road through Aby. Visible today from this road is the first Lincolnshire acquisition of the Woodland Trust. Kew Wood, of just less than one acre, was planted in 1982. Aby is fortunate also to possess several stretches of ancient hedgerow supporting a rich variety of flora and fauna.

The northern entry into Aby is marked by an old girder bridge, part of the East Lincolnshire branch of the London and North Eastern Railway. The line was completed in 1848 and since its closure in 1970 has become something of a private nature reserve with the new owners having planted trees or simply allowed nature a free rein. The proximity of the railway line provided the reason for the naming of Aby's only hostelry, the Railway Tavern, which has an interesting collection of railway memorabilia.

In view of the Tavern, across a field, is the redundant Aby church, a wood and corrugated iron construction built in 1888 on the site of the original All Saints' church. The latter was demolished in the 17th century, the stones and font bowl being taken to neighbouring Belleau by Sir Henry Vane for his mansion there (now also demolished). The chalice from the original All Saints' is now kept at Belleau, also the bell from the 1888 building which had previously belonged to HMS *Bacchus*. A very attractive Wesleyan chapel built in 1895 now provides the only facility for divine worship within Aby. An earlier chapel, erected 1825, has been converted for use as a village hall. At the heart of the village is Aby's charming primary school. The two original classrooms were built in 1852 at a cost of £400. The architecture epitomises the popular image of a rural village school, complete with picket fence and mature trees shading the playground.

In many ways Aby is still a village of traditional character. It has a combined post office and store which doubles also as a general information centre. There are several old established families resident and Aby has not yet become a dormitory settlement. However, most of its crafts and tradespeople have been lost to the modern way of life, the village blacksmith presenting therefore a fascinating anachronism with his old fashioned skills and his earthen-floored shop, a source of wonderment to many a passer by.

Alford 🌿

Alford is an interesting place with a population of just over 2,000. There was a settlement here in pre-Norman times and also a place for crossing the beck. In the Domesday Book the name is given as Alforde. When the beck was turned into a water catchment drain it became known as the Wold Grift.

The importance of the village's situation was soon recognised when William of Well became lord of the manor of Alford. He obtained a charter in 1283 for a market on a Tuesday and for two annual fairs at Whitsun and in November. These were very popular until 1939, the bull fair continuing until 1972. The cattle market established in 1911 was closed in 1987. There was a railway, much used, opened in 1848 but closed in 1970 when the Grimsby to Boston line was demolished.

Alford church was built on the site of an earlier building, demolished in the 1350s. There is a very fine 14th century wooden screen, a richly carved dark oak Jacobean pulpit and a large alabaster monument of the late 1660s to Sir Robert Christopher and his wife. A large south porch with a room above, still used, was probably the original home of the school founded by Francis Spanning in 1566. In 1576 Elizabeth I granted a charter naming it a grammar school. After several moves the Queen Elizabeth Grammar School was established in its present site in 1881 and enlarged to become co-educational in 1959. The church fell into a very bad state of repair and in the 1860s Gilbert Scott undertook extensive restoration, adding another north aisle, raising the height of the tower by six feet and adding eight Ancaster stone pinnacles.

There are several attractive thatched houses, including the manor house which is owned by the Civic Trust and houses the headquarters of the LSHTNC. There are also some very good examples of Georgian houses, still private homes. In November 1785 the first Lincolnshire Stuff Ball was held in the Windmill Inn and this became so popular that in 1790 it was transferred to the Assembly Rooms in Lincoln.

Alford still has a beautiful fully operational five-sailed windmill, built in 1813 of brick, tarred over to ensure that it was waterproof. The sails, the ogee cap and the fan tail are all painted white and it is visible for many miles. It is open to the public at weekends in the summer and occasionally at other times. This mill is the only survivor of four windmills working here in 1900. It has had a more or less continuous commercial life and is now publicly owned and still capable of grinding four or five tons of grain a day.

Within a radius of about five miles of Alford there are many small villages and hamlets with interesting houses and churches, architectural remains and 'lost' villages.

At Haugh a line of very ancient yew trees leads to a farmhouse built on the site of an old mansion. Close by is a tiny ancient stone church with a Norman doorway and Jacobean memorials.

Well is a small village with a fine red brick Georgian house, now a school. It overlooks a lake and the slope of a well planned park which leads to a small church built in 1733 to resemble a Grecian temple.

Ulceby is a small village on the banks of a stream. A red brick church with a bellcote also serves the hamlet of Fordington where the humps of a 'lost village' can be clearly seen. At Claxby two long barrows are clearly visible. One has been much damaged by a chalk pit, now owned by the Lincolnshire & South Humberside Trust for Nature Conservancy, as is the nearby Hoplands Wood.

Willoughby lies on the edge of the marsh and has a large sandstone church with some Saxon and Norman work. There are also interesting modern windows depicting the life of Captain John Smith, who was born in the village in 1579. He emigrated to America, where his life was saved by Pocahontas, an Indian princess. He later became Governor of Virginia.

Bilsby is a fast growing village with a much restored church that has some interesting earlier work. The tower has old brick battlements. Markby is the site of an old Augustinian (Black Friars) priory. The little thatched church has box pews and fragments of early stonework. At Hagnaby there was once a Premonstratensian (White Friars) priory, fragments of which remain in the nearby farm.

A tiny greenstone Georgian church can be found at Hannah, on the last piece of rising ground before the coast. There are box pews, a marble font and a three-sided Communion rail. Belleau also has a greenstone church, greatly rebuilt in the 19th century but containing the remains of a much older building and an effigy of a crosslegged knight. Nearby there is an interesting and very well restored octagonal brick dovecote.

Allington 🌿

In old documents the name of the village is spelled Adelington or Athelyngton, indicating that it was a Saxon settlement. Its name means the home of the family of Athel, a Northumbrian prince.

From Domesday until recent times it was a combination of two parishes, East and West Allington, supporting two Anglican churches and a Methodist chapel for a population of 300 to 400. St James's church, which was always connected with the neighbouring village of Sedgebrook, was demolished in 1947. All that now remains is the graveyard and a stone cross erroneously marked 'St Andrew's'. The Methodist chapel was demolished in 1938. The present parish church of Holy Trinity, originally of West Allington, displays a variety of architectural styles demonstrating repairs and extensions over the centuries. The poet, George Crabbe, was rector here from 1790 to 1814.

The village was owned by the Welby family for nearly 200 years, hence the name of the public house, and changed very little until the estate was sold after the Second World War. The provision of mains water in 1948 and mains sewerage in 1952 paved the way for new building. The school, opened in 1907, was extended in 1983 to accommodate the children from Sedgebrook school.

The cross on the village green is a market cross, Allington at one time having been second only in importance to Grantham as a market.

On the Sedgebrook road is a stone-capped chalybeate spring known as the Salt Well. Before the mains water supply was connected this was an important source of water for farm stock.

Today the population of over 500 is served by a church, a school, a general store-cum-post office, a public house and a village hall. Situated between the A1 and A52 the village gives easy access to many large cities. As a consequence few of the inhabitants both live and work in the village, but it is by no means a 'dormitory', but a lively and interesting place to live, with 14 clubs or societies catering for all ages from toddlers to senior citizens. It even has its own bi-monthly newspaper.

Alvingham 🐝

Alvingham lies in valuable agricultural land nearly four miles north-east of Louth and is part of the area known as Middle Marsh. Though quiet today and largely unspoiled, it was here that Gilbert of Sempringham, son of a Norman baron, founded his priory in 1130 next to the site of the earlier Saxon church of AD 550, details of which are to be found in the Alvingham Missal in the Bodleian library. The priory remained active until the Black Death claimed most of its inhabitants, as the plague pit at Cockerington, a mile away, bears witness.

Many of the old priory stones are still to be found in the fields of Alvingham and the two churches of St Mary and St Adelwold remain to this day in the one churchyard, declared by Hugo of Wells, Bishop of Lincoln in 1215 to be a 'perpetual vicarage' served by one vicar. St Adelwold's, in which today's services are held, lay almost derelict for nearly 100 years and was restored in 1933, while St Mary's is cared for by the Redundant Churches Trust. Two churches in the one churchyard earns the village mention in many guide books but visitors are unprepared for the unique approach over a bridge by one of the country's few remaining working watermills and through a farmyard. High heels are not recommended in winter but those who continue through the old churchyard will find themselves beside the river Lud, undisturbed now except by birds, but once an active part of the Louth Navigation Canal along which ships came, past Lock Farm to the basin in Louth.

The mill has supplied the needs of the village for many hundreds of years and is mentioned in the Domesday Book. It has been lovingly and beautifully restored by its present owners and is open to the public at advertised specific times when it can be seen fully working. The village still has a working blacksmith whose skills nowadays are devoted to metalcraft, close by the old forge, though the latter is temporarily out of use. Another link with the past is the stocks, made and put in place during Jubilee Year on the site of the originals. The pottery was once the wheelwright's shop and draws a steady stream of tourists, who are welcome to watch the hand-throwing and hand-decorating, in fact the whole process, before buying the goods in the showroom and visiting the tearoom.

Although in recent times newcomers have been attracted from areas far away from Middle Marsh, the rural character of the village has been maintained. The active Victorian Methodist chapel, the village hall with its many associated activities, together with the store and vegetable shop, each owned by the same family for generations, help to retain the individuality and agricultural charm indicative of one of England's still largely unspoilt counties.

Amber Hill 🐟

Amber Hill became a civil parish in 1880. The village consists of two parallel roads and drains linked by Chapel Lane.

There is a church, St John the Baptist, and primary school. The two chapels have now been converted into family homes. Most of the 5,478 acres of the parish are put to agricultural use, but there are a large number of cottage industries in the village. The children from Holland Fen and Hedgehog Bridge attend the school since the closing of their own.

A pumping station was built in the late 1960s to help drain the land, superseding the old water-wheel, the remains of which can be seen on Maryland Bank. The two ha-has are also situated along Maryland Bank. In the middle of the village is a little shop and post office.

This peaceful little village seven miles north-west of Boston continues to survive despite modern day pressures.

Anton's Gowt 🐟

Slightly to the north-west of Boston lies the village of Anton's Gowt, reached via the B1184. The word 'gowt' means sluice, but the more common name locally is Anton's Gowt Lock. This is a haunt for both anglers and boating enthusiasts, many of whom frequent the river Witham and the Oak Tree public house during the summer.

Sadly much of the past is no more. The Methodist chapel, built by the Doughty family in 1852, is no longer in evidence. Its centenary was held in June 1952, in the carpenter's shop of the Burn family, and the service was conducted by Mr H. Doughty of Lincoln, who was 95 years old. It actually closed in 1964, when it still had 18 Sunday school scholars.

In the past there were many different forms of business in the community, including the Malcolm Arms (now the Oak Tree), the railway, village shop, petrol pump, milk and paper rounds. Now there is a post box, telephone box, kennels, a dog and cat cemetery, potteries and a game farm, plus many other businesses.

The Lincoln to Boston boat race, held annually, attracts local and far off visitors, either to support a particular crew or from general interest. Ideally summer is the best time in the village, as most people are very keen gardeners, and the flowers are a sheer delight.

The village has grown since the 1960s, extra land having been made available for homes, for people seeking a rural environment.

Bardney 🐾

The question 'Do you come from Bardney'? means not 'Are you a Bardneyite?' but is a way of saying 'You've left the door open', referring to a legend from Bardney's 7th century abbey, the resting place of King Ethelred of Mercia. After the monks of Bardney Abbey had closed their door to the bones of the saint and martyr Oswald, they received a wrathful divine message by a pillar of light and they vowed never to close the door again! This abbey was restored by Gilbert of Ghent in 1087 and devastated by Henry VIII in 1538. Excavated by the local vicar Rev C. E. Laing in 1909, the work was completed and written up in an archaeological journal by Harold Brakspear FSA.

The village stands at a crossroads looking westwards over the fens to Lincoln Cathedral and eastwards to the Wolds and coast, surrounded by rich agricultural land.

Bardney and its hamlet Southrey are now home to some 2,000 people and are dominated by the very modern factory of British Sugar, processing half a million tonnes of sugar beet during the season.

The 15th century church of St Laurence, the early 18th century Handcock's Almshouse and Kitching's Charity School and school house are at the centre of the village around the green, with the recent addition of an appropriate memorial to the 9th Squadron of the Royal Air Force who were stationed here during the Second World War. There is a new primary school, replacing the two former schools, the Wesleyan day school and the Kitching's Charity School. The old Wesleyan premises now house four rural workshops.

Of the five public houses those by the river Witham, The Jolly Sailor and The Railway Hotel, remind us there was once a busy wharf and railway station. The Nag's Head, The Angel and The Black Horse cluster around the Stocks Hill tree. The village has a village hall, youth club, playing field and pavilion, and has recently twinned with La Bazoge a small town near Le Mans.

Bardney Station

16

Barkston le Willows 🌿

Barkston le Willows is an attractive village lying on the river Witham four miles north-east of Grantham.

Mentioned in the Domesday Book in 1086, the village at that time was called Barchester. The survey listed a Roman camp and four mills in the area.

The church of St Nicholas is on the site of previous churches, dating back 700 years.

In 1837 a free school was opened in the village, although there already existed a small school, the gift of the Newton family, for six poor children, dating from the 17th century.

In recent years there have been a number of new houses built but the old village still stays the same with a thriving village hall.

In November a Craft Fair is held in the village hall which attracts a great number of local people. There is a hotel/restaurant and the local hostelry The Stag also serves meals.

Barrowby 🌿

Barrowby stands on an escarpment over 300 ft above sea level overlooking the Vale of Belvoir. The name Barrowby means 'settlement on a hill'. An archaeological survey in 1971 revealed flints and pottery dating back to the Neolithic age and subsequent occupation by the Danes and the Normans. The Domesday Book records the village name as Bergebi.

The church dates from 1215, though there was probably a previous building on the site. Its commanding position overlooking the vale makes its spire visible for many miles to homecomers. Its greatest treasure is the font, a richly carved model of the 14th century. The stem is hollow and inside can be seen a carving of a monkey. The oldest tombstone in the churchyard is dated 1772. The fine lychgate was presented by the Rev George Earle Welby to celebrate his golden wedding. There are five bells in the church tower, which are rung on many occasions.

The rectory, built in Elizabethan times, is a handsome building but over the years it has been reduced in size and extensively altered. It has been sold for conversion into a home for the elderly.

There are a number of properties of historical interest, including

Barrowby House built in 1691, the Old Hall built on an early medieval moated site, the Malting House dated 1636, The Gables and Holly House. There are also several cottages dating from the 17th century.

Chapel Lane, next to the post office, was the site of two chapels, one for Wesleyan Methodists and one for the United Reformed congregation.

The reading room was donated by Canon Welby in 1899 to commemorate his 51st year as rector. It is a valuable facility for the village and whist drives, parties, jumble sales etc are held there today.

The building of modern estates started in 1960 and has continued unabated since. The population of over 2,000 makes Barrowby one of the largest villages in Lincolnshire. However, the increased population means that there is a thriving extended primary school, a good bus service and a small supermarket, post office and an excellent butcher. The public house, the White Swan, has darts, pool and golf teams and the Scouts and Guides have their own modern premises.

There is a thriving cricket club and football club on the Low Field and an annual gala involving all the village organisations is held on the village green.

Belton ✳

Belton is a picturesque village, three and a half miles from Grantham, boasting Tudor bedehouses.

Belton House was designed by Sir Christopher Wren and completed by James Wyatt in 1685 and was the home of the Brownlow family for almost 300 years. Lord Brownlow was Lord in Waiting to Edward VIII and some of the souvenirs on display in the house relate to the abdication in 1936. The house, which is surrounded by beautiful parkland, is now owned by the National Trust and is open from Easter to October each year. For the visitor there are nature trails and an adventure playground for the children amongst the delights to enjoy.

Many memorials of the Brownlow family can be found in the church of St Peter and St Paul, the tower of which dates from about 1200.

On the outskirts of the village is Bridgewater House, which was at one time the home of the Fitzherbert Wrights, grandparents to Sarah, the Duchess of York. Older residents remember her visits there as a child.

A most delightful garden centre is situated in Belton which attracts many visitors from miles around.

Planning permission was given in 1988 for the building of a country hotel with conference and leisure facilities which will include a golf course, swimming pool etc. The hotel will be built near woodland on the approaches to the village on the Grantham side.

Binbrook 🐑

Binbrook is in an idyllic setting in the North Lincolnshire Wolds, mentioned in the Domesday Book as Binnibroc. The population peaked in 1861 at 1,334 and has continually declined since. The village once had a weekly market but records refer to this being sold to Caistor many years ago.

The village was noted for the purity of its water in the 19th century and for being built on a brook abounding with trout. The brook, which flowed through pasture between the manor and the church, was piped in in 1989 to allow for building development.

The manor, a listed building, is early 18th century with late Victorian additions. Worthy of note are the beautiful windows and the urns on the gate-posts. The oak panelling in the hall was done by Mr H.W. Thompson, a local carpenter, in the late 19th century.

The parish church of St Mary and St Gabriel was consecrated in 1869 and united the two former parishes. St Gabriel's was in ruins in 1822 – its churchyard, now grassed over, makes a pleasant quiet corner in which to sit. St Mary's, a small plain structure, was pulled down in 1867. The present church is often referred to as the 'cathedral on the Wolds', and was described by Geoff Bryant, an authority on churches in the region, as 'a super job by Fowler – a good example of a 19th century church pretending to be medieval – perfect in every detail'. The spire was extensively renovated during the time Canon Richard Crookes was rector.

In 1988 a new stained glass window was installed, a gift to commemorate the RAF presence from 1940 to 1988. The old rectory is a short walk away and the present rectory lies on the outskirts of the village.

Methodist gatherings date from the mid 18th century, first with open air meetings and in private buildings. The quaint Ranters chapel still stands, since used as a garage and workshop. The Wesleyan (1815), Primitive (1836) and the Free Methodist (1856) chapels also have other uses. The Free Methodist chapel was later greatly reduced in size and in more recent times was bought and restored as a community hall to commemorate the coronation of Queen Elizabeth II. It is known today as the Queen's Hall. The present Wesleyan chapel was built in 1877.

The hill farmers depended on the village for drinking water and Cornelius Stovin in his *Journals of a Methodist Farmer 1871 – 1875* noted that his men went down to the village for water. The pump on the Grimsby Road is built on a ramp to enable water carts to fill up.

The school erected in 1842 was enlarged in 1871 to accommodate 200 pupils. The fine modern school built on to this had close links with families from the nearby RAF base, and in 1988 a gift, a section of a tail fin from a Lightning was mounted on a plinth in front of the school. Opposite the school is a small memorial to the Royal Australian Air Force – a wreath is laid each year on Anzac Day.

The police station or lock-up (now a private residence) was built in 1852. The superintending constable lived there and there was a room for magistrates' meetings – the Rev John Huntley was the local magistrate. Petty sessions were held there from time to time. The two Binbrook constables were assisted by constables from Ludford, Tealby and Thoresway.

Life though was centred round the Market Place, High Street and Back Lane with their blacksmiths, beerhouses, builders, bakers and millers, carpenters, carriers, ropery, reading room, shops, shoemakers, tailors and wheelwrights. A 200 year old blacksmith's shop was pulled down in 1989. The white cottage in the Market Place with a cartwheel outside denotes the premises of Mr Walt Appleton – wheelwright, carpenter and undertaker. A market trap built in 1899, owned and used by Mr Robert Stark, carrier, was restored by students from the Lincolnshire College of Art conservation course and is now displayed in the transport gallery of the Museum of Lincolnshire Life.

In 1851 East House was the home of one of the then two surgeons, and many doctors have practised from there since. Water was pumped from a well in the front garden to a tank in the roof – the well was filled in during the practice of Dr Lawn. Dr Lawn, as doctors before him, carried out minor operations on the kitchen table – this stopped at the formation of the National Health Service in 1948.

The Granby was the venue for property auctions in the 19th century, while at the Plough the early meetings of the St Mary's Court of Foresters (established in 1839) were held in 1852. The annual dinner was also held at the Plough.

No trace remains of the Temperance Hall (1840) or the sail windmill, but the water mill on the outskirts of the village (now a private residence) was the scene of cock-fighting, which earned it its name, 'the cock mill'.

Blyton

Blyton is a long narrow village occupying more than a mile of the busy A159 Gainsborough-Scunthorpe road.

Parts of the church, dedicated to St Martin, date from Norman times, though its most unusual feature is the collection of the flags of the Allies in the First World War. At the end of the war in 1918 the vicar wrote to each nation requesting its flag; the letters received in reply have been retained, including the one from Buckingham Palace explaining that the Royal Standard could only be displayed when the King was present so his request must be refused!

The popular children's authoress, Enid Blyton, was descended from the local de Bilton family, who were wealthy wool merchants.

Braceborough

Braceborough in rural Lincolnshire, recorded in the Domesday Book 1086, and reached only by narrow lanes, boasts its own spa, where once Spa House had its spa room for taking the water. At one time the water was bottled and sold.

King George III is rumoured to have taken the water and to have been treated by Francis Willis MD who resided at Braceborough Hall. Dr Willis ran a private asylum for mentally ill people at Shillingthorpe, an ancient and remote hamlet of Braceborough.

It is believed Dr Willis kept his trap in the stone trap hovel at the entrance to Manor Farm. A trap hovel is so called because it has doors either end. One drove into the trap hovel with both doors open and led the pony out at the front leaving the trap inside the building.

Today Braceborough consists of approximately 40 cottages, farms and newer houses. Three pre-enclosure farms, Manor Farm, Ivy Farm and Berry Farm still exist in the village centre.

The friendly village community is served by St Margaret's church, the post office and a village hall. The village hall was once the school and was built by the Willis family in 1870 and left in trust, 'to be used for the education of adults and children of the labouring, manufacturing and other poorer classes in the parish of Braceborough'.

Bracebridge Heath

Bracebridge Heath, a community of more than 3,000 inhabitants, straddles the main roads from Lincoln to Sleaford and Grantham. Although it is only two miles from the centre of Lincoln, the village is part of the District of North Kesteven.

There is a small industrial estate on the Sleaford Road but the largest collection of buildings is St John's Hospital. The main building, with its Palladian front, is a listed building. Having cared for the mentally ill for decades, the hospital is closing and many of the patients are now being cared for in the community.

Cross O'Cliff Court, where the superb cricket pitch is the home of the village cricket club, houses the headquarters of the North Lincolnshire Area Health Authority.

The foundation stone of St John's church was laid by the Bishop of Grantham on 21st September 1907. For many years the church was within the parish of All Saints', Bracebridge, one and a half miles away down a rough and steep path. On 1st November 1971 parish status was achieved and the Rev Harley Moreton was instituted as the first vicar.

The Viking Way, the long distance footpath from the Humber to Rutland, enters the village at the top of Cross O'Cliff Hill and continues along the Cliff edge until the Waddington parish boundary is reached.

Branston

Branston, which dates from Saxon times, is situated in open countryside four miles from Lincoln on the B1188 to Sleaford and its centre is the old village with winding lanes and stone-built cottages. It has increased in size rapidly over recent years with the building of large housing estates to a population of nearly 4,000. There are many well-walked country footpaths with views of the Wolds and the cathedral, and a guide to these can be bought from the local library.

The village is well catered for in terms of schools, playgroups, evening classes and recreational activities. There is a large hotel, The

22

Branston High Street

Moor Lodge, a library, the Waggon and Horses public house and the Home Guard Club which was formed during the Second World War. The new village hall was opened in 1981 and is situated in the extensive recreation field which includes tennis courts, football and cricket pitches, a bowling green and a children's play area. Three medical practices have surgeries in Branston and there are adequate shopping facilities. A regular bus service operates to Lincoln and Sleaford.

The tower of All Saints' church was built by the Saxons and there are some interesting pew ends, one of which has a carving of a pig playing the famous Lincolnshire bagpipes. The church suffered considerable damage by fire on Christmas Day 1962 and it is now a pleasant combination of old and modern architecture. For 211 continuous years a member of the Curtois family was the incumbent and there are three former rectories, one of which has a cock-fighting pit in its garden.

There are two Halls; the first, which was built in 1735, burned down in 1903 whilst the annual Goose Supper was being enjoyed at the then new Hall. The latter, used as a hospital for some years, is now a retirement centre and the old Hall has been rebuilt as a private house.

The picturesque stream which flows through the village is home to many ducks and the occasional trout. This stream provided the power for the former waterworks with a huge waterwheel which pumped the water to the large houses. The wheel is still in existence.

Brant Broughton

Brant Broughton lies near the foot of the Lincoln Cliff, and its church spire, one of the most elegant in the county, draws visitors like a magnet.

Despite having lost such picturesque features as the stream that once bordered the High Street, and several mature trees, Brant Broughton remains an attractive village with only a limited amount of intrusive development. Along the High Street and scattered down the lanes where wide verges once provided grazing, are some fine brick and stone houses. They date mainly from the 18th century, and several incorporated much earlier and humbler dwellings, which then became the kitchen quarters as their owners moved up the social scale.

The forge in the High Street is still connected with the Coldron family, blacksmiths in the village for many generations, and noted in the past for high quality wrought ironwork. There are examples in buildings as diverse as the local parish church, Lincoln and Peterborough Cathedrals and Castle Drogo, one of Sir Edwin Lutyens' masterpieces, as well as in many houses in the area.

St Helen's church is described by Henry Thorold in *Lincolnshire Churches* as 'without doubt one of the most glorious of all Lincolnshire churches... like a medieval dream.' It has two splendid porches with a number of carvings, some of which were regarded by a contributor to the *Gentleman's Magazine* in February 1809 as 'too indelicate to be permitted to occupy one of your plates'. Inside there is a fine 15th century nave roof resplendent with carved angels.

Residents at the old rectory included William Warburton, a noted scholar of his day, and a friend of the poet Alexander Pope. Warburton was rector from 1728 to 1779 but an absentee from 1745, retaining the living when he obtained other appointments, the most important of which was as Bishop of Gloucester in 1759.

Two famous huntsmen of their day were also residents at the rectory. The first of these, Sir Richard Sutton, lived there with his uncle and namesake after inheriting the Brant Broughton estate from his grandfather in 1802, when he was three years old. He hunted successively with the Burton, the Cottesmore and the Quorn, and shortly before his death in 1855 was spending £10,000 a year on the last of these. In 1820 the Reverend Henry Houson became rector. He was connected with the Suttons by marriage, and remained at Brant Broughton until his death in 1873. He hunted with the Belvoir, and was said to be 'the most noted of the Belvoir parsons', still capable of leading the field when he was over 80.

The Quaker meeting house which gives one of the lanes its name was originally a thatched barn belonging to Thomas Robinson. He and his family fled here from London in 1665 to escape the plague, and spent some time in quarantine in Clog Close, the site of the primary school in Mill Lane. Meetings of Quakers were held illegally at Beckingham and Robinson had some of his property seized as a punishment for attending them. By 1701 the laws against Dissenters had been suspended for some years, and Robinson and his wife Sarah gave their barn for use as a meeting house. Although the building has been altered over the years their initials may still be seen above the door.

Brant Broughton's other places of worship, both dating from the early 19th century, are the Methodist chapel at the corner of West Street and Mill Lane and the Wesleyan Reform chapel in Maltkiln Lane.

Education was first provided for poor children in the village as the result of a Vestry meeting in January 1731, and a variety of schools followed. The Old Hall and a building behind Woodbine Cottage were both boys schools, but there was also provision for girls at Stone Cottage and Yeoman's Cottage. In 1852 and 1871 respectively the Methodists and the Church of England established their own all-age mixed schools, and there was considerable rivalry between them. Children at the Church school had extra holidays on Shrove Tuesday and Ascension Day and the Methodist children had to be pacified by longer playtimes or being allowed to leave early!

The log books of both schools tell of the problems faced by their head teachers in trying to improve attendance. The rector, the Reverend Arthur Sutton, attempted to improve the situation at the Church school. On Friday afternoons he gave a metal token to every child with a full week's attendance. At the end of the year the tokens were each redeemed for one old penny. In 1898 this cost him over £8 and another year over £10. But the scheme seems to have lapsed after a time for reasons which are not stated. Perhaps the rector found it too expensive, or it may have been that a new attendance officer was more effective!

Burgh le Marsh 🎵

Burgh le Marsh is a thriving community, constantly expanding with new developments, situated a few miles east of Skegness on the A158.

Outdoor activities consist of football, cricket, bowls, fishing and a Rifle and Pistol Club. For those who enjoy walking there are many pleasant walks along country roads and field paths. Recently a picnic area has been provided at the Grand Pits. At the village hall there is something going on nearly every evening, and the venue has proved so popular that the old schoolhouse was bought as an annexe. This includes a new library.

Unfortunately there is no railway station now in Burgh as this closed down in 1970, but there is a Railway Museum which has proved popular with holidaymakers. There is also a windmill which is still operated in the summer with voluntary help.

Amenities include a school, post office, garages, a dairy, a doctor's surgery, a library, a coal merchant's, several public houses and various shops. There is a library service for the housebound and meals on wheels.

There are two rest homes for the elderly, Burgh Hall and St Paul's. More dwelling houses are being put up as the population increases and a new school has been built for the same reason. Flats now stand where once the old cattle market used to be.

There are three places of worship in Burgh. The parish church, dedicated to St Peter & St Paul, is an impressive building of Portland stone, with a fine tower.

Caistor 🎵

Caistor, a small market town which retains the atmosphere of a village, is situated high on a western spur of the Wolds, off the A46 road between Great Grimsby and Market Rasen. It is a place of steep, narrow, winding lanes, of flights of steps and little passageways and of magnificent views, including that of Lincoln Cathedral in the far distance.

Caistor was a Roman camp and many vestiges of the Roman occupation have been found. Parts of the wall which surrounded the camp are still in existence and they also constructed Ermine Street which passed nearby. Another important road is the ancient High Street which runs from Caistor to Horncastle.

Caistor men were involved in the Lincolnshire Rising of 1536, which was a reaction against Henry VIII's attacks on the Church, and there is an effigy of Sir Edward Maddison, who played a prominent part in the rising, in the church of St Peter and St Paul. This beautiful church is of the Norman and Early English periods. The glass and nearly all of the church plate is modern and the church houses a Gad Whip. This whip is connected with a custom that took place on Palm Sundays in the past whereby a whip, a purse containing silver and some pieces of wych elm had to be presented at Matins.

Other places of worship are a very fine red brick Methodist church and a small, well kept Catholic church. There are three schools, a joint Church of England/Methodist primary, Yarborough secondary and the grammar school. The latter was founded in 1630 and has facilities for boarders.

The Market Place is most interesting, having several late 17th and 18th century buildings. There are no earlier buildings due to the 'great fire' in 1681 which destroyed over half the town. The many different roof levels add charm and character as does the Victorian pump with its coat of arms. Leading from the Market Place are areas still named the Butter, Corn and Horse Markets.

The gems of Caistor are its fresh water springs, Syfer Spring in Fountain Street perhaps being the best.

A good deal of building has taken place in Caistor of recent years and that near the centre, notably George Mews, has been built in a fitting style. Industrial development is mainly on the lower outskirts of Caistor and this includes the well known firm 'Cherry Valley' who despatch ducklings and their by-products worldwide.

Of the public houses the Fleece Inn is perhaps the best placed scenically. In the past it was known for its Palm Sunday Fair when thousands of sheep were sold. A small market is held in Caistor on a Saturday and the various shops in and around the Market Place supply most needs.

Carlby 🐚

Carlby is a small village lying halfway between Bourne and Stamford with a population of approximately 300.

The nearest shop/post office and pub are a mile away at Essendine. However, activities are thriving due to a new village hall built in 1987 by voluntary labour, financed by a council grant plus many large fund-raising events to top up the required funds. The new hard tennis court and an outdoor bowling green are part of the newly developed playing field complex.

St Stephen's church is in an attractive rural setting in a very well kept churchyard. It has a medieval wall painting which was partially uncovered during church restoration in the 1930s. In 1983 many village ladies worked colourful tapestry kneelers and cushions. Canon Robertson, vicar for ten years, gave an attractive hand-turned elm Pascal candlestick in 1987 which enhances the simple beauty of the church.

Caythorpe with Frieston

Caythorpe with Frieston is a very friendly village on the A607 within easy reach of Lincoln, Grantham, Sleaford and Newark. There is a good hourly bus service between Grantham and Lincoln, and on market days buses go to Sleaford, Newark and Boston. The surrounding countryside is pleasant and varied and there are many picturesque houses with colourful attractive gardens.

The village is fortunate to have an abundance of amenities. There are two mini-supermarkets, a butcher's shop, a fish and chip shop which also delivers fresh fish, a post office, a school, a church, three public houses all serving food, a surgery and three resident doctors, a garage, a hairdresser, a dressmaker and Margaret's Studio featuring hand-painted china. Residing in the village are plumbers and decorators, builders and electricians – to name but a few.

At one end of the village is a complex of warden-controlled bungalows with an adjacent community centre. Near to the church is a residential home for the elderly. The village hall is used to capacity for various social events and there is a spacious playing field with a large pavilion for the cricket and football clubs – a children's play area is incorporated.

Near to the village is Caythorpe Agricultural College which provides various courses throughout the year. Plants, pot plants, cut flowers and farm produce are available to the public.

Recently at Frieston, the landscaped Lakeside Farm Fisheries for trout and coarse fishing has been opened.

All in all, a desirable village to live in, and last but not least – a resident policeman to keep order!

Chapel-St-Leonards

Chapel-St-Leonards is a 'village-by-the-sea' with an extensive sandy beach and a real village green. It is a few miles north of Skegness, off the A520.

There are two Women's Institutes, a branch of the Royal British Legion and several other recreational organisations.

The Methodist chapel and St Leonard's parish church – which is thought to have the only red-towered spire in the country – provide for the religious needs of a population of around 2,700.

Several pubs, two hotels, a good variety of shops and an octagonal village hall complete the picture. The village hall was provided by public subscription and is 'managed' by a committee elected annually.

Upwards of 50,000 visitors come to Chapel-St-Leonards each year, proving its popularity as a holiday village, particularly for families with children.

Cherry Willingham

Cherry Willingham lies three miles east of Lincoln on the south-facing slope above the wide valley of the river Witham. The parish varies in altitude from 15 ft above sea level on Willingham Fen to 100 ft at the top of the slope.

Lincolnshire has several Willinghams so our village has Cherry has the first part of its name, probably because there was once an orchard called Cherry Holt just below the church.

At the turn of the century a local newspaper described Cherry Willingham as 'one of the prettiest villages in the near neighbourhood of Lincoln, in winter it is rather shut off from the world, as the village lies off the high roads'. What a changed world those words evoke.

The village has spread outwards from the original settlement behind the church, where Iron Age remains have been found. A series of long narrow medieval fishponds is still in existence. A Roman villa was discovered just above the flood plain of the Witham, which was not embanked until late Victorian times.

The fen is the source of bog oak, large trees dragged out of their graves in the peat and hauled away to the clay soil for safe burning. If the fen peat is set alight it can smoulder for weeks.

At the time of the Domesday survey there was a church and a priest and two fisheries worth 32 pence yearly. The manor house stands opposite the church. After the Conquest the manor was owned by the Marmion family until the early 18th century when it passed into the ownership of Thomas Becke, whose memorial is in the church. The present church of St Peter and St Paul, an excellent example of Georgian architecture was consecrated in 1753. It is built of high quality Ancaster limestone and stands on a commanding mound.

At the foot of this mound is the spring-line, a problem in some gardens, but at one time the water was famous for the care of weak eyes. There used to be an iron ladle fastened to the flagstones by the side of the spring, but this and the pump that replaced it have disappeared.

Cherry has a farmstead in the centre of the village where a handsome herd of Lincoln red cattle can be seen in the crewyard throughout each winter. Every year a Harvest Festival service is held in the barn.

The village did not conform to the classic ancient pattern whereby every village had its woodland for timber and fuel. In fact Fox Covert is a tiny wood; however the turbary on Willingham Fen provided peat.

In 1821 Cherry had 89 residents living in 16 houses. In 1842 it was described as 'an indifferently built village' of 111 inhabitants. By 1901 the population had risen to 145, most of whom were limestone miners working on the outskirts of Lincoln, agricultural labourers or employees of the Great Northern Railway,whose Lincoln – Market Rasen line bisected the parish in 1849. In 1921 there were 186 residents, but 30 years later this number had risen to 445 because of the ease of commuting to Lincoln.

The village still did not possess a public house and it was not until the Witham View and Cathedral View estates were built in the late 1950s and 1960s that the Cherry Tree and the Wishing Well were provided. The population is now over 3,000 and an estate of more than 300 houses is being built on the poorly drained land behind the church. Each of the two big estates has a group of shops, but most shopping is done in the supermarkets or ordinary shops 'in town' or in Nottingham for the grander purchases.

Although there is a busy railway line there has never been provision for a station. In former days passengers walked to Reepham or took the ferry to Washingborough to board a train.

There was no school in Cherry Willingham from the early 1920s until the opening of infant and secondary schools in 1965. It was 1976 before a junior school was added.

A recent development is our twinning with Le Grand Luce, a small town near Le Mans. Each year a coach party of French or English makes the 350 mile journey to stay with their host families and enjoy a contrasting style of life. Lasting friendships have been formed and as a result we have come to know each other better.

Claxby 🐚

Claxby is a small village nestling at the foot of the Wolds. There have been people living in this area for 2,000 years, but the name Claxby comes from the time of Danish settlement in the 8th century. The second syllable 'by' means farm or village and the first syllable is the name of a man, 'Klaka'. The village is mentioned in the Domesday Book as 'Clachesby'.

The present church of St Mary dates from the 13th century. Opposite the church is a public house called The Coach House, which has been converted from an old barn attached to the village manor house. Further into the village is a hostel used by walkers along the Viking Way, a long distance walk from the Humber into Leicestershire. This hostel was originally the village school. The post office is in the centre of the village and is situated in an old converted Methodist chapel. The houses in the village are built in a mixture of brick and traditional stone. There has been some new development in recent years with infilling of some plots.

Claxby is five miles equidistant from Market Rasen and Caistor. Both market towns are used for shopping as there are no shops in the village. The local children are bussed to school in nearby Holton-le-Moor and Market Rasen.

The surrounding area is mainly farmland growing mixed crops, and raising cattle and sheep. The village has changed in the last 25 to 30 years from a very rural way of life, with the majority of people now working in nearby towns.

The village is situated in an area of 'outstanding natural beauty'. There are wonderful woodland walks, hill walks and an abundance of wild animals and flowers. In the spring the hedgerows are full of birds nesting and snowdrops and celandines peep through the hedge bottoms.

The village gardens themselves are very picturesque with most people keeping a tidy plot. Many people grow their own vegetables and keep chickens, ducks etc. The winters can be long and hard and travelling becomes difficult at times. But the great beauty of the summer months makes up for this.

Coleby

The village of Coleby is situated seven miles from Lincoln, to the west of the A607 Grantham to Lincoln road. This attractive small village is superbly positioned on the edge of the Lincoln Cliff and panoramic views are enjoyed by walkers along the Viking Way which runs through the village.

A large part of Coleby was designated a conservation area in 1977. There are many interesting old buildings in the network of lanes, some still enclosed by the limestone walls which are a feature of this village. Two stone wellheads stand on the east green, near the Methodist chapel.

Coleby Hall, on the edge of the village, was built in 1628 for Sir William Lister, on the site of an earlier Hall. Although much altered since that time, part of the original structure is retained in the present building. In the grounds of Coleby Hall is the Temple of Romulus and Remus, which was erected on the instruction of the owner, Thomas Scrope, in 1762 'In memory of Liberty and Pitt' and was designed by the architect, Sir William Chambers. (Coleby Hall is not open to the public).

The parish church of All Saints is the centrepiece of the village. Following the Norman Conquest a new church was built on the site of an earlier Saxon one, the Norman builders retaining the lower part of the Saxon tower and building upon it. As with most churches of such great age many alterations have taken place in the ensuing centuries. The crocketed spire was added in the 15th century. There is much to see inside the church, including the drum-shaped late Norman font, which is still used for baptisms.

In the 14th century land and property in Coleby was acquired by the Swynford family, who also held estates in Kettlethorpe. The family's most famous member was Katherine, wife of Sir Hugh Swynford, but better known as the mistress, and later wife, of John of Gaunt, Duke of Lancaster.

Colsterworth with Woolsthorpe

The villages of Colsterworth and Woolsthorpe, population 1,094 adults, lie half a mile to the west of the A1, seven miles south of Grantham and 13 miles north of Stamford. Colsterworth is raised upon a slight limestone ridge with the river Witham running below on the western side and bisecting the two villages. The ancient village of Twyford has been engulfed by the expansion of Colsterworth to the south but the name is preserved in the names of certain houses. At one time Colsterworth lay astride the Great North Road, but was bypassed when that highway was realigned and renamed.

The nucleus of the village lies along the High Street where, in the hey-day of the coaching trade there were numerous inns, ten at one time, now reduced in number to one only. The old coaching stops have been transformed into houses or business property (The George House : The Sun Pottery) or demolished completely. The White Lion alone now serves the population, standing opposite the parish church of St John the Baptist, the origins of which go back to Saxon times, as indicated by the herring-bone stonework in the chancel. The fine Norman arches were preserved during the Victorian period of renovation, of which this church is an outstanding example. The surrounding churchyard has been closed for almost a century but is kept in good order by the Parish Council.

Although the oldest dwellings are of limestone, which requires constant attention for its upkeep, brick homes of the 1920s and 1930s are interposed amongst them, giving the village a rather patchy appearance. During the 1970s a large estate was built on ground previously belonging to Colsterworth House, an imposing mansion now completely obliterated. All the land between the village and the A1 will soon be covered as a new housing estate is completed. Newcomers, in the main, tend to commute to work out of the area, some as far as London.

The local council, anxious to preserve the separate identities of Colsterworth and Woolsthorpe, bars the building of new property between the two villages, although much infilling is taking place as large gardens are split up and odd plots, overlooked for years, are utilised.

The village has a post office, a surgery, hairdresser and resident police constable. Local shopping is catered for by the Co-op and by the farm shop, while mobile shops include two greengrocers, two butchers and a

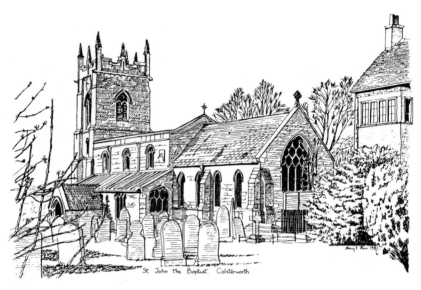

St John the Baptist, Colsterworth

St John the Baptist, Colsterworth

fishman, and the County Council library and travelling bank call once a week. The primary school, for children of this and neighbouring villages who are bussed in, has approximately 120 pupils divided into five classes.

There is little employment in the village itself. During and for some time after the Second World War, work was available at the ironstone excavations, but since they ceased operations and the site was filled and levelled, only Vaculug, a tyre depot, and Salvessons, the cold-food store, offer local employment. Otherwise farming, the traditional occupation which not so long ago absorbed all the available workforce, and part time jobs at one of the quick food restaurants which are springing up along the A1, are all that the village has to offer.

Woolsthorpe, although attached to Colsterworth by administration, has a character all its own, being smaller and quieter. It is famous as the birthplace of Sir Isaac Newton in 1642. His home, Woolsthorpe Manor, attracts visitors from all over the world. The village hall was built as a result of an appeal in his memory and is named after him. He was christened in the church of St John the Baptist, where a copy of the entry in the register is to be seen.

Coningsby 🦚

Coningsby is a large, thriving village on the A153 Midlands to East Coast road. It is within easy reach of Horncastle, Boston, Sleaford and Lincoln. The river Bain flows alongside the village, which is on the edge of the Lincolnshire Fens. In the Domesday survey, Coningsby was a prosperous place with ten fisheries.

Some of the best and earliest vegetables are grown in the sandy soil of the parish. Sixty shops and businesses serve the community.

St Michael's church is famous for its one-handed clock, fascinating to horologists, as the 16½ ft painted dial, pre-mid 17th century, is reputed to be the largest of its kind in the world. The unusual mechanism consists of hand-crafted iron wheels, stone weights and steel ropes.

Although a church probably existed here pre-Conquest, the tower on which the clock is painted is 15th century. This tower is unusual in that it stands outside of the church, with a beautifully arched carriageway underneath and an unglazed rose window to the west.

The south porch, with a parvice chamber, is decorated with a stone monkey at its apex, a reminder of the animal which escaped from a travelling circus, snatched up the Earl of Coningsby's baby heir, and dropped him to his death; the last of the Coningsby line. The parvice room is entered from the church.

Inside St Michael's are many interesting features including a Dutch national flag draped behind the altar of the Royal Air Force chapel. A Dutch lady Resistance worker covered the bodies of three British Servicemen during the Second World War with this flag.

The head of a scold, wearing a bridle, is forever silent in stone above one of the nave columns. The church registers date from the 16th century and people with the same surname as the first entry still reside in the parish.

Other listed buildings are the Lea Gate Inn, where there was once a toll bar. The bracket for the lantern which guided travellers over the undrained fens is still attached to the corner of the house.

The Baptist chapel, with burial ground at the rear, is said to be the second oldest Baptist place of worship in the country. The Methodist chapel in Dogdyke Road is an Elizabethan house and the old rectory, in private ownership, is a fine example of a medieval timber-framed house.

The Royal Air Force station, Coningsby, is the base of Tornado aeroplanes of Strike Command, the first line of defence. Plane spotters converge around the perimeter to pursue their hobby, as aircraft of many kinds and countries come and go.

The Battle of Britain Memorial Flight is housed on the airfield, manned by volunteer former fliers, and is open Mondays to Fridays to the public. Thousands of people flock to the RAF Open Day each year, in June. Proceeds are shared among various local charities.

Each year a Christmas meal and entertainment are organised by the Commanding Officer and staff for Senior Citizens around Coningsby and Tattershall, and each year members of the RAF co-operate with various other village bodies when the Christmas tree lights are switched on in St Michael's churchyard and hot soup is provided after the carol service.

Other leisure activities are catered for by various groups. Cruises to Boston or Lincoln may be taken from Belle Isle on the river Witham. There are quiet roads for horse riders and walks of various distances along river banks or by fields. A new children's playground was recently opened near the junior and infants school.

Corby Glen

Corby Glen – the name formally adopted in 1955 to avoid confusion with the town of Corby, Northants – is a village of approximately 450 inhabitants, situated on the Bourne-Colsterworth road. The village and surrounding parish of 2,799 acres are situated in wooded hilly countryside in a largely farming area.

The village boasts a market cross. There are three churches, a primary school and a secondary school, three pubs, a post office, a doctor's practice, a butcher's shop and two general shops. In addition to a children's play area, there is a bowling green.

During the redecoration of St John's church in 1939 discovery was made of a remarkable series of wall paintings, said to be the finest in Lincolnshire. In medieval times few men could read or write and it was common practice to illustrate stories from the bible by paintings on the church walls. As progress was made from one story to the next the paintings would be covered with whitewash and further pictures painted on top.

The Willoughby Memorial Gallery and Museum is housed in what was formerly a free grammar school. A trust was founded in 1965 by the Earl of Ancaster in memory of his son who was drowned in the

Mediterranean. There is a well stocked library and reading room and several times a year exhibitions of art and related subjects are staged for the public.

Perhaps Corby Glen is best known for its annual sheep fair, which owes its origin to a Royal Charter of 1238. At one time sheep were brought in by rail and on foot from as far away as Suffolk, Oxfordshire and the Scottish border. The fair was a notable event in the calendar, being at the end of the farming financial year (tenant farmers in hard times would be forced to sell their sheep in order to settle rent arrears). Over the years there has been a decline in the number of sheep brought to auction at the October Fair, but it is still an occasion when reunions of families and friends take place. October 1988 saw the 750th anniversary of this event and a week of displays and celebrations took place, culminating in the sheep fair auction on the Monday.

Like most of the small villages within easy reach of Grantham and therefore within commuter distance of London, there has been a shift in the population with an emphasis on the building of executive houses, but nothing will change the peacefulness which is the core of the village of Corby Glen.

Deeping St James

In 1220 Est Depinge was granted a charter for a market to be held on the high ground on the western side, where now the modern roads A15 and A16 meet; so the two villages of Market Deeping and Deeping St James were formed.

Deeping St James took its name from the priory church of St James and St Benedict, which was founded in 1139 by Baldwin FitzGilbert, Norman lord of the manor. The village green and lock-up must be two of the smallest in the county. The lock-up, now known as the Cross, is a small square building, once used as a meeting room and later on to house village drunks.

The river Welland was used as a highway for trade when barges went their way to Stamford and Market Deeping. Along Bridge Street, just before the locks, there is an old house with a canal window on its first storey, used to sight the traffic on the river. Many improvements have been made along the river because of the disastrous floods, and today it is a favourite spot for fishermen and angling clubs from many parts of the country. The river has always played a part in the social life of the village – in the 1930s the Bathing Belles, led by District Nurse Lanham, believed in a daily dip for health; today there are canoe races, duck (plastic) races for charity and tug-of-war contests across it.

In the Linch Field along the Spalding Road a Bronze Age cinerary urn was found, which is now in the British Museum. There are many links with Roman times, including the Car Dyke crossing with the river Welland.

Although the roots of village life were mainly in farming, and the yearly Agricultural Show is still held, down by the railway station is the Mere, with extensive willow beds and well known to wildfowlers.

The road to Peterborough and the south goes over the river by the old three-arch bridge, which is very narrow and has small niches each side for pedestrians to step into to avoid the traffic. Along Bridge Street, by the bridge, is the Cave Abdullam Baptist church, founded by Reverend F. Tryon, a former vicar at the church, who disagreed with Church doctrines and built and endowed his own place of worship.

The village today has large new estates and is classed as a dormitory village, but, in spite of this, the old and new mix well to form a busy working and social area. Modern amenities are shared with Market Deeping – almost on the boundary we can boast a modern health centre, police station, fire station and library. A leisure centre is amalgamated with the comprehensive school, there is still a Village Carnival Day and, in spite of the new estates, there are many pleasant and enjoyable places to walk around.

Deeping St Nicholas 🐝

The village of Deeping St Nicholas in south Lincolnshire is one of the longest villages in the country, extending some five miles along the busy A16 south of Spalding.

The name Deeping means 'a place in the deep meadows, subject to flooding' and the parish of St Nicholas in Deeping Fen lies so low that it would not exist without a careful system of drainage. Efforts to keep the water away extend from the reign of Queen Elizabeth I when a petition was presented to drain the fens. During the 1630s the Earl of Bedford and Sir Philibert Vernatti carried out much effective work in draining the area with the cutting of Venatts Drain and Counter Drain, and the improvement of North and South Drove Drains. Windmill pumps met with only partial success and it was not until the establishment of steam pumps in the mid 1800s that an efficient drainage system was obtained. This work is continued today by an electric pumping station at Pode Hole.

With the proper drainage of the fens in 1845 a church was built and dedicated to St Nicholas and this gave its name to the village which came into existence in about 1850.

The reclaimed land is of exceptional fertility and farming was once the main occupation together with associated trades of saddlery, wheelwrights and cart makers. But as mechanisation came, more and more people had to look for work outside the village in nearby Spalding and Peterborough. Cereals and sugar beet are the main crops, potatoes used to be grown in large quantities and the potato railways were in great use. These light railways ran from the main road to the bottom of the farms, usually by the side of dirt tracks. Horses were used to pull the trucks laden with corn or potatoes. Sadly these are a thing of the past along with horses and wagons, their place taken by tractors and lorries.

The construction of the Lincolnshire loop line as part of the old Great Northern Railway, which runs through the village, provided rapid transport for the rich farm produce to the towns and cities. Until 1857 the main line from London to the North ran to Peterborough and thence through Deeping St Nicholas, Spalding and Lincoln to Doncaster. The station's name of Littleworth differs from the village name. The trains no longer stop here and the station buildings have been converted into offices.

The parish church, although not built until 1845, was designed by the Sleaford architect, Charles Kirk, in the style of the mid 14th century with a dramatic spire, and built of Ancaster stone. It has a peal of six bells. There is also a thriving Methodist church, built in 1867. In the early part of the century until the outbreak of war in 1939, on one day of the year the Sunday school children used to parade the village in horse-drawn vehicles known as Jersey waggons, returning to the chapel for tea, then sports, followed by a dance. It was the highlight of the year for the children.

At one time there were six public houses in the village but today only the Blue Bell and the Plough remain in business. Of the two post offices only one remains and one small village shop and a butcher's shop.

The parish of Deeping St Nicholas includes the small village of Tongue End which is some seven miles away by road. Here, during prolonged periods of hard frost, land adjacent to the river Glen is flooded and ice skating championships held.

Denton 🌿

Denton is a delightful cluster of cottages, together with a church, a chapel, the school, a post office, village hall, public house and manor house. Lincolnshire is usually associated with flat country, but Denton is in a sheltered vale and cosily situated in a corner of South Lincolnshire. The Main Street calls for the engagement of a low gear and Church Street too rises gently, with St Andrew's church crowning its highest point.

The Norman church is built of the local 'yellow' stone, and when floodlit by the sun St Andrew's is a magnificent golden building. On entering the church, the many stained glass windows throw warm welcoming shadows across the aisles, and the soft furnishings (a serene blue in colour) are very pleasing to the eye. The registers date from 1558, and nowadays the rector is shared with three other parishes.

The Methodist church can be found off the Main Street. This building is about 150 years old and is cared for with love. Denton school is a solid stone building. Already many generations have received a good basic education here, and the school looks set to stand guard over many succeeding generations of Dentonians.

The community centre (known as the village hall), the public house, the post office, and not forgetting the Women's Institute, are perhaps the nucleus of the present day village. The post office has been in the same family for five generations.

The nearest market town is Grantham to the east, with Melton Mowbray to the west. Re-entering Denton from Grantham, the first view is of the ornate gatehouses standing guard over Denton manor house drive; these were built in 1898.

Going back many centuries, Denton was part of the land granted by William the Conqueror to his Standard Bearer, Robert de Todenni – hence the name Denton. The original village was built around the church and village green (now the garden of Denton House). Park Lane is said to have been the first village street, and its continuation can still be traced through the park.

Within the manor grounds, there are three lakes, one of which has a grotto which shelters St Christopher's Well, the water of which was said to have health-giving properties. The middle lake of the three has a small island which is now the home of numerous Canada geese, whose cries fill the air as they noisily pass over the village. These lakes feed the quite large Denton Reservoir. The Grantham-Nottinghan Canal also passes through the outskirts of the village, but this waterway is now used only by anglers.

Until comparatively recently (the early 1950s) the only water supply was from numerous springs in the parish. There were pumps in the streets and gardens, and the water was sparkling clear though very hard. Making a necessary visit to the pump was excuse enough for a neighbourly gossip: now there's just the lonely tap!

The majority of Dentonians now work outside the village, but this was not always the case. Not so very long ago, Denton belonged almost entirely to the Welby estates, and the squire was the largest employer, in the mansion (now demolished), in the manor grounds and on estate work. There is still a squire, but he now lives in a much smaller manor house and the estate employs but few men. Many others were in the employ of the farmers, but modern farming machinery means fewer labourers in the fields. For many years there were ironstone workings, when large numbers were employed by Stewart & Lloyds, but this too came to an end.

The village was once part of the Forest of Kesteven, and trees are still a feature of Denton, many of which grow to a great height. Many new trees have been planted and these too are showing remarkable growth. The horse chestnuts are particularly beautiful in Denton and visitors come to enjoy their glorious blossoms each June.

There is said to be a Denton ghost, a dark figure on horseback, dressed in a cloak and tricorn hat, and seen by John Watson of Nottingham on the night of 28th January 1967. Mr Watson slammed on his brakes to avoid a collision and the horseman vanished. The apparition was also seen by a Mr Shenton a few days later.

Donington

Donington, once a small but thriving market town in the Lincolnshire Fens, lies almost equidistant from Spalding and Boston and is inhabited by around 2,500 people. Now designated a major village, it was referred to as Donnictune in the Domesday Book. Then a hamlet, its salt works were worth £1 per year and land was valued at 60 shillings. Its prosperity in the Middle Ages is evident from the size and grandeur of the church. Mainly 14th century, the church bears evidence of much earlier masonry.

Australians visit St Mary and the Holy Rood throughout the year to pay homage to their hero, Captain Matthew Flinders RN. His memorial is in the church and, since 1980, thanks largely to the generosity of the Australian Governors, a stained glass window commemorates his exploits.

Matthew, son of the local doctor, is said to have been fired with a desire to go to sea after reading *Robinson Crusoe*. Fearful of voicing this ambition to a disapproving father, he printed his request on to the surgery slate! He was the first person to circumnavigate Australia and bestowed many Lincolnshire place names on that land. During his 40 year life span he achieved a great deal and endured much hardship including over six years captivity on Mauritius during the course of his explorations.

In commemoration of Captain Flinders, the heads of all the Australian States make an annual pilgrimage to Lincolnshire in early March – first to Lincoln Cathedral and then to a service at Donington followed by tea served in the Hall. Children look forward to the occasion and to the souvenirs always distributed by the visitors.

Matthew's home, now demolished, stood on the edge of the Market Place. In his lifetime markets were held for the sale of flax and hemp which went to London to be made into ropes used by the Royal Navy.

The High Street was once alive with horses for the Horse Sales held in May and afterwards the animals were taken to the railway station en route for new homes – such was the horses' terror of the sound of the steam engines that many were blindfolded before being persuaded to

Donington

42

embark. Sadly, the station has been closed for a number of years although moves are afoot to try to reopen it. Today, an adequate bus service caters for those without cars.

The Market Place is surrounded by shops supplying every commodity to a growing community. At the end of the High Street stands Cowley's School, established in 1719 by Thomas Cowley, the village's greatest benefactor. It was once a grammar school with a boarding wing, attracting pupils from far and wide. History was made in 1871 when the school was one of the 15 teams to enter for the very first FA Cup. It was forced to withdraw from its fixture with Glasgow's Queen's Park Rangers because of the distance involved and the cost which amounted to £2 per boy! In 1972, as part of the FA Centenary Celebrations, the match was played in Glasgow and was covered by the national papers and the media. School representatives attended the FA banquet in London and were given souvenirs of the event. Today Cowley's School is secondary modern catering for about 500 children.

Situated in the heart of Tulipland, Donington holds an annual Flower Festival timed to coincide with Spalding's Flower Parade. The church is decorated and hundreds of meals are served to the travel-weary by volunteers including members of the Women's Institute.

Donington has seen many changes in the 1980s. Land which once grew bounteous crops has been snapped up by builders to provide houses and the days when everyone knew everyone are over. Although most of the 'old characters' are gone and the community spirit is somewhat fragmented, time will meld the old and the new to forge further links in the chain of village history.

Dyke 🌿

Dyke, two miles north of Bourne, is generally known as a village but is really a hamlet as it has no church. It grew up on the west side of the Roman canal, the Car Dyke, which some say was a means of communication in those times but others maintain was a catch water drain. According to the Domesday Book, Oger the Briton, no doubt of French extraction, owned land in Dyke in 1086 and it was divided into arable, pasture and woodland. The people of Dyke were mostly peasant workers. In the Middle Ages there was strip farming with a three year rotation of crops. Considerable attention was paid to drainage and land to the east of the Car Dyke was being reclaimed.

So a mainly agricultural community grew up with allied trades supporting it. Landowners centred in Bourne seem to have owned the land at Dyke. Over the years bigger houses were built for the farmers and landowners and stackyards, stables and cowsheds were built around them. There were some houses with thatched roofs but only one remains. This one, called Redmile Farm, may date back to Elizabethan times, as perhaps does one other with its mullioned windows and 19 inch thick stone walls.

D. Birkbeck, in his book on Bourne, says that in 1868 there was a small National school and divine service was also held there. Around this time Jane Redmile, who lived in the village, was so concerned about the local children that she started a Sunday school for them in her own kitchen. Eventually after several moves to other houses she built a school at her own expense (£60) and the number of children attending rose to 80. However the Bourne/Sleaford railway line was built and her building was demolished.

The keen members of the Baptist church living at Dyke but worshipping at West St Bourne were determined to build a chapel for themselves at Dyke. There was great excitement when it was completed in 1879 and then in 1895 an adjoining schoolroom was built. This was used on Sundays but leased to the Local Education Authority as a day school until it closed in 1980. There is also a small privately owned Methodist chapel but unfortunately this has had to close down for lack of support.

Many trades were practised in the village in the 19th century and the first half of the 20th. There were two general grocery shops which sold a variety of goods including underwear. There was a smock mill built in 1845 and a bakehouse built in 1865. For many years the Summerfield family ran this business and bread was delivered to the villagers by pony and cart. There was also a forge and blacksmith's shop and for many years Bill Robinson was the blacksmith.

The village was well served by public houses but only one survived, the Crown, which has been altered and is now a very popular small hotel renamed The Wishing Well. At one time there was a cobbler, a butcher and a carpenter-cum-undertaker. One of the first buses to run in the area was that owned by Bill Walpole, who lived opposite the top shop. His father built Engine House, which has a traction engine depicted on the date stone, and Joseph Walpole travelled round to farms with his engine and tackle when corn threshing was in progress.

During the Second World War children from Hull were evacuated to the village accompanied by a teacher and his wife. Many lasting friendships were made and some marriages later celebrated. At the end of the war a Welcome Home Party for those who had served in the Forces was held and all the village joined in. This was the first of many annual village parties which drew the inhabitants closer together.

The character of the village has changed over the years. Farmers have cut down on labour and increased their mechanical aids so that in contrast to pre-war years only a minority of the population is engaged in agriculture. For some years a bus from a local factory collected workers and the drift from the land increased. Now with the aid of the motor car workers commute to Bourne, Spalding, Stamford, Peterborough and even further afield. The characters in the village have largely disappeared. We think back to Walter Willy Mills who kept the village shop and was a great talker, Shep Kendal who retired to bed early and amused himself by singing old folk songs to the delight of passers by, Nurse Rouse in her long black skirts who pickled onions in her spare time and old Ben Laxton who swept the roads and chatted about the good old days.

There are some good tradespeople in the village – electricians, carpenters, a builder and a plumber. There is only one village shop but we have retained the post office. A tractor firm has moved into the centre of the village, an engineering business is run from Engine House and there is a garage. At the bottom of the village, Meadow Drove Kennels has built up a good reputation.

In 1927, 1930 and 1952 groups of council houses were built and later a group of council bungalows called Stubbs Close after the councillor, Cecil Stubbs, was built. More recently there has been private building since the 1960s. For the most part people have integrated well but now more development has been proposed many of the villagers are fearful of the subsequent changes to the environment and the village community. A Residents Association has been set up to safeguard the interests of the village and it is hoped that Dyke will still retain its identity and will be a peaceful and friendly village in which to live.

East Keal 🐝

East Keal is about two miles south of Spilsby along the A16, on the edge of the Lincolnshire Wolds and fens. The village dates back to Saxon times, and the site to the Stone Age. It is still a farming village with sheep in the Wolds fields and crops on the fens, very much as it has always been. It is only the views that have changed. The wild marsh and meers of the fens are now a flat patchwork of fields and the odd line of trees for a windbreak, with buildings scattered here and there.

In this small rural village there was once a church, a chapel, a school, a butcher, baker, blacksmith, carpenters, pigman, wheelwright, coal merchant and post office with grocery shop, as well as the smallholdings and farms, but sadly many of these have gone. However the crocuses, snowdrops and daffodils which line the side of the road in spring, the post office and grocer's, garage and garden centre, and a couple of pick your own fruit farms make it still a small friendly community.

The stone built church of St Helen is one of the main attractions. It has a peal of six bells, a south facing porch, a chancel, nave and aisles, and also a rather unusual font. Around the base of the octagonal bowl are seven faces and facing the door next to the pillar a bare bottom. One can only assume that the mason had a sense of humour!

On the edge of the village to the east there is an ancient well, on the border with Hundelby. It is called the Virgin's Well and has never been known to dry up, very important in earlier times. It is much covered over now and hidden in the Twentylands Plantation. It is a pleasant place to go for a walk, one of a number around the village, taking in the fields and hedgerows of the Wolds and the ditches and dykes of the fens, all rich in wildlife.

If one decides to take a walk up the hill towards Old Bolingbroke and Mavis Enderby and then looks back, the view is really quite breathtaking. On a clear day one can see as far as the coast, and you can also see the churches of eight parishes from this spot. Just by the lane end there is a road sign that used to say 'To Old Bolingbroke and Mavis Enderby', to which a wit with a spray can had added 'a Son'. It has gone now but there are still those in the village with a sense of fun, one of them in the village post office. Mr Middleton sells ice-creams. Red coloured ones are Squashed Beetle, the green ones are Squashed Caterpillar. One dare not ask what the rest of the flavours are called.

East Kirkby

The village of East Kirkby is situated between Skegness and Boston. It is mainly agricultural, growing potatoes and sugar beet as its main crops. The 14th century church of St Nicholas is outside the village where the old village used to be. During the Second World War an American air base was here and it is remembered in a recently opened Air Museum and in services on Remembrance Sunday.

There is only one general store and post office combined. There is a public house, the Red Lion, and cafe and two petrol garages. At present there is a primary school but unfortunately this is likely to close in the near future, owing to the small number of children attending.

A thriving nursery and fruit and vegetable store on the main road is a hive of activity in the summer and a further garden centre is doing good business on the fens. There is a small company making tools for wood-carvers and turners which despite its size has a world-wide reputation and trade.

On the same site an enterprising business is being run selling antique tools, also on a world-wide basis. There is also a company selling and repairing fridges. The village hall has in the last few years been renovated and is now in demand for village activities and private parties and wedding receptions. The manor house has been opened as a residential and retirement home and is proving very popular.

Fishtoft 🌿

A rapidly expanding village lying two miles east-south-east of Boston with a population of 5,291, Fishtoft adjoins the parishes of Skirbeck and Boston to the west and north, that of Freiston on the east and the sea bank on the south. The name of this parish is written in the Domesday Book as Toft. 'Toft' is generally understood to imply a hill or higher ground, which correctly applies to this parish when compared with the surrounding countryside.

The 19th century local historian Pishey Thompson states in his account of Fishtoft that a creek of considerable magnitude once flowed from near the church to the neighbourhood of the present Hob Hole Pumping Station, and clear traces of this creek can still be seen to the east of the Cut End Road. This creek may have been there as early as Roman times. A Romano-British farm settlement excavated in the 1960s was situated on the west bank of the creek, the Roman levels being only 15 inches below the current surface. Going even farther back in time, Stone Age flint artefacts have been found on the land lying immediately south of the church.

Apart from its beautiful church dedicated to St Guthlac, Fishtoft has only one historic building still standing, Rochford Tower. This fortified manor house was built of brick in the early 16th century and is contemporary with Tattershall Castle. Sometimes known as Kyme Tower (members of the Kyme family are buried in Fishtoft church) it is an impressive red brick tower with corner turrets and embattled parapet standing just south of the inn on the A52 Wainfleet Road. It is supposed that the present tower stands on or near the site of the ancient Richmond Tower of Fenne. There was a chapel of Fenne dedicated to St Michael in the 1300s, situated immediately north of the inn. Hence the name Church Green Road, which runs north/south between St Guthlac's church and the chapel of Fenne. The hamlet of Fenne dates back to the 13th century.

Rochford Tower is square in plan having an octagonal turret on its south-east angle which contains a flight of 70 steps, communicating with the three upper apartments. These floors and the one time lead-covered roof have disappeared through decay. On the plastered walls of the first and second storeys of the tower can still be discerned religious paintings of angels and a coat of arms, probably that of the Kyme family.

The Rochford family must be one of the oldest families in Lincolnshire and they can be traced back to the Norman Conquest. Alan Rufus, Earl of Brittany and Richmond, a nephew of William the Conqueror, was the first subject in the Kingdom of England and next in rank to the Royal Family. According to the Domesday survey, Earl Alan held land in Skirbeck, Fishtoft, Benington, Leverton, Leake and Wrangle. He died without issue in 1089.

There are a number of ancient sites in Fishtoft. In 1733 Vincent Amcotts held a mansion and eight acres of land in the part of Fishtoft known as Hilldyke. A mansion known as The Guildhall stood on the site of the present Red Cow Inn, the property of William Blanchard in 1709.

Lord Mountville's house stood on the site of the present Fishtoft Manor in 1724. A site on the west side of Church Green Road opposite the New Grange was known as Rice ap Rice and was the home of the first Mayor of Boston, Nicholas Robinson, in 1544.

A site immediately to the north of St Guthlac's church was the home of the Pagnell family who settled in Fishtoft in the middle of the 15th century. This family later moved to Boothby Pagnell, hence the name. Willoughby House to the north of the A52 Wainfleet Road and to the west of the road to Hilldyke is the site of Willoughby Hall, which stood on 61 acres of land held by the lords of the manor in the 17th and 18th centuries.

Towards the southern end of the village is the site of a monument to the memory of the Pilgrim Fathers who attempted to sail from Boston to Holland in order to find a more favourable scope for their particular religious views. In 1620 came the historic journey of the Pilgrim Fathers to America – vanguard of a great tide of migration in which the town of Boston was to be closely involved.

Fiskerton

Bordering the northern bank of the river Witham five miles east of Lincoln, this large parish comprises a comparatively small village straddling the Lincoln to Bardney road, the Longwood of some 250 acres, Short Ferry and a former airfield of the Second World War.

The Domesday Book mentions three fisheries at Fiskerton, a clear indication that the village received its name as 'home of the fishermen' in ancient times. Recent excavations by archaeologists unearthed substantial remains of a wooden pier and several bone needles undoubtedly used in repairing nets, which have been dated back to the Stone Age. A wooden canoe, a large cache of looped and socketed axe heads and medieval jewellery have also been discovered, proving thousands of years of continuing habitation.

In this county of memorable old churches, Fiskerton boasts a splendid example dedicated to St Clement where Christians have worshipped for a thousand years. The half round interior of the tower; the hanging, brass oil lamps converted to use electricity, and a plaque to the memory of those who served at the wartime airfield are of particular interest.

The population of under 1,000 is well served by a modern primary school, two public houses, a newsagency and a busy post office. The Victorian school has been enlarged and transformed into a warm and comfortable village hall which is in regular use by organisations catering for all age groups and interests. The adjoining master's house has been adapted for use by the Scout and Guide groups, and field sports are enjoyed on the Manor Paddock in the heart of the village.

Farming is largely arable with some sheep. The Longwood lies east of the housing, beyond Short Ferry where the river Barlings Eau converges with the Witham and here are sited a further public house/restaurant and boating marina.

Particularly attractive in the summer time when yellow water lilies abound along the village stretch, the river, running alongside the entire length of the parish, is a popular spot for anglers, walkers and nature lovers. Here too an iron pedestrian bridge provides the only crossing of the river between Lincoln and Bardney. Fiskerton is noted as having one of the few known ponds in Great Britain where the Great Crested Newt breeds.

Little remains of the wartime airfield apart from short lengths of runway, however the headquarters and underground operations room of Midland Area and No 15 Group Royal Observer Corps and United Kingdom Warning and Monitoring Organisation are now on that site. Originating in former RAF buildings, Tanya Knitwear Factory has substantial new buildings housing modern machinery and providing employment for 200 people.

It is believed that the saying 'Getting the wrong end of the stick' originated in Fiskerton centuries ago when it was the custom for land to be conveyed between the steward and tenant at the manor court by each grasping one end of a 6 ft long pole.

Present day travellers to Fiskerton can be assured that they will not be getting the wrong end of the stick when they visit this cheerful place.

Foston

Five miles north of Grantham a toll bar marked the southern boundary of the village of Foston. The toll keeper's house still stands, now a ruin and much altered from its original design which gave the keeper a window north and south to look for traffic, with a door between them for the collection of charges.

The road is the A1. Also known as 'The Great North Road', it connected London with Edinburgh and several coaches a day passed up and down during the 19th century. Local farm traffic was reasonably heavy, and indeed it would seem that the coaches, circuses, gipsy caravans and other travellers caused so much vibration that the picture frames rattled on the cottage walls.

There were three inns. The Duke William stood at the junction with Allington Lane; the Black Horse was in the centre of the village, its former stables now converted into three attractive cottages; the Black Boy was just down the hill on the Newark road. They catered mainly for local trade. There is reference in *Nicholas Nickleby* to an incident which could be connected with the Black Boy. Charles Dickens is thought to have stayed there on his way to investigate the Yorkshire schools scandals. 'Mr Squeers' may have known it too! Increasing road use finally made a bypass necessary and gave more peace and security to Foston.

Foston in the Domesday Book is written 'Fozton'. The local pronunciation is 'Fosson'!

The village was at its most prosperous in the 19th century when the population grew to 550; until recent years it was under 400. Local needs were supplied by the farms who were the largest employers, others were bakers, tailors, shoe and harness makers, and a four-sail post mill. The mill had had several sites in its long life from 1624 to 1966. In its last years it was a landmark in a holding beside the A1.

The Roman settlement was beside the river Witham, which is the village boundary. It was an important walled fort and quite early coins have been found there. How soon or for what reason the settlement moved uphill after the Romans left in the 5th century is uncertain. Perhaps the Saxon farmers who moved to the top of the small hill preferred a better view of possible enemies. The A1 has a long history of marching armies.

Foston is a linear village with no clear centre or green. At a junction the A1 continues to Newark and a road – a very old road – runs down to the ford on the Witham, which may be the reason for the Roman settlement there.

Foston village

The church of St Peter stands near the road junction. It has several Norman features including one of the finest chancel arches, cut in chevrons, in the county. Evidence of Saxon work has been revealed on repair work. The patron of the joint living of Long Bennington with Foston is the Duchy of Lancaster, ie HM the Queen. The church clock was the village's recognition of the Diamond Jubilee of 1897 and even today with radio signals, clocks and watches universal, its occasional 'moods' are noted and commented on.

A feature of the church is the set of brass candlesticks on wooden staves which were inserted in a circle placed strategically at pew ends all down the nave and elsewhere. They were the only means of lighting for many years and are probably Georgian and very attractive.

'Fosson Feast' was very eagerly looked forward to – it was held on a Saturday nearest to St Peter's day, 29th June, and marked the Patronal Festival. The beer no doubt flowed freely in those days of unrestricted drinking; roundabouts and various amusements and side shows attended.

The school, dated 1847 and replacing an earlier one, sadly closed in 1987, but a play school is held three mornings a week in the village hall.

Fotherby

Fotherby is situated along the A16 road between Grimsby and Louth at the foot of the Lincolnshire Wolds.

Approaching the village from either the north or south one's first view is of the broach spire of St Mary's church, which dominates the village. The church was built in 1863 on the site of an earlier church, the walls are of chalk and sandstone lined inside with red bricks and sandstone bands. There is a 15th century font, a medieval piscina and three 17th century bells.

The six almshouses have long been a feature of the village. Built on the site of an old vicarage in 1867 by the generosity of Everitt Allenby, they have provided sheltered housing for over 120 years. The exterior of the almshouses has not been altered, though the interiors are now modernised.

Everitt Allenby was born at Manor Farm in 1794. He later left the village for London where he became a successful businessman. He died in 1868. He provided money for the chancel of St Mary's church when it was built in 1863.

Fotherby is a village most people pass through. If the traveller leaves the main road and takes the country lane to Fotherby Top, 350 ft high, on a clear day his journey will be rewarded by the most wonderful views of the long stretch of marshland and of the sea as far as the Humber and Spurn Head.

Linger a while by the common, a peaceful spot to enjoy the sights and sounds of nature in the countryside on a summer day.

Frampton 🐚

Frampton is four miles south of Boston. A noticeable feature of this fen village is its trees. No other village around the Wash can boast so many.

At Mill Hill crossroads the copse is a colourful sight in springtime with snowdrops and daffodils. To the west, behind a brick wall, is Frampton House, built in 1792 by the Tunnard family. The mound on which the mill had stood was taken down and used to fill in the road to Frampton House. The poor road conditions from here to the parish church, and the distance involved, resulted in the Tunnards building St Michael's church in 1863.

On Ralphs Lane a commemorative plate marks the site of the gibbet where in 1792 Ralph Smith was the last person to be hung in chains in the Boston area. He had murdered Gentle Sutton.

Middlegate Road leads east from Mill Hill to Frampton village. The old school was built in 1818 and extended in 1877. Notice the attractive sundial and inscriptions over the doors.

Behind Parks Farm an early 19th century round, brick dovecote is a typical fenland building, although nowadays few remain. The blacksmith's home and workplace is now a white-washed cottage, 'The Old Forge'. Probably many of the interesting field gates and fences in the area were made here.

Thornimans Lane is one of the few lanes bounded on both sides with hedges. Multon Hall Cottage, built in the mid 17th century, is reputed to have been the home of the tithe collector for the manor of Multon.

Near the war memorial stand several attractive estate cottages, one of which is thatched, an unusual sight in this area. Another has intricate dog-tooth brickwork with a decorated porch.

Frampton Hall, standing in its own park, was built in 1725 by Coney

53

Tunnard. Rabbits appear on many parts of the buildings and railings as a pun on his name. (See the rabbit on the chandelier he gave to the church). The house was built with three storeys, uncommon at that time. The later east wing has the arms of the Moore family who married into the Tunnard family.

St Mary's church is mentioned in the Domesday survey. The earliest parts are the tower and broach spire which are late 12th century. The earliest gravestone dates from 1693 and is near the east window.

The manor house is 18th century, as are several large farmhouses in the village. The Moores Arms, dated 1690, is named after Col Moore who lived at the Hall. At Church End the imposing H-shaped brick house with walled garden is Cotton Hall. Built in 1689 its first occupants were the Cotton family, possibly related to John Cotton, Governor of Massachusetts and commemorated in the Cotton Chapel of Boston Stump.

The Greenwich Meridian is crossed on the way to the sea banks and salt marshes. Frampton Marsh is a bird sanctuary. A local delicacy growing here is samphire. Boiled and pickled in vinegar it is eaten with cold ham.

Freiston

A typical fenland village lying three miles to the north of Boston, with a large and beautiful church. St James' is the remains of a priory founded on this site in 1114 as a cell of Crowland Abbey. The present church is about a quarter of its original size and apart from the 12th century pillars, the arches and 13th century porch, very little remains of the original building. The legend which has grown up around the font is worthy of mention. The cover of this, sculpted in an elaborate tracery from oak, is said to be the work of an apprentice. The carpenter himself having delegated the task to the apprentice, flew into a rage upon seeing the magnificent piece of work and murdered the young lad. The ghost of the apprentice is believed to haunt one of the village lanes.

The priory, which is now a private dwelling, is mainly 17th century with Georgian alterations.

White Loaf Hall, so called because it was here that the first white loaf of bread was baked, has a varied history, having been a monastery and also a prison at some time. It is believed that one of the monks trying to produce a finer loaf of bread sieved the flour through his socks in order to rid it of roughage! The old bread oven is still in existence today.

The Plummers hotel situated out on the Freiston shore was once a thriving complex, together with the Marina hotel which is no longer in existence. Horse races used to be held on the shore between Freiston and Butterwick. From 1900 to 1936 many people came from the Midlands and Yorkshire to stay in the two hotels and enjoy a spot of shooting on the marshes. The Marina had 23 bedrooms. Stalls were set up on the sea bank and buses ran from nearby Boston. However, the sediment built up rapidly with the two daily tides. The Marina was no longer a viable proposition so it closed. The Plummers is today a public house.

Freiston shore was used during the Second World War as a practice area for bombing raids, particularly a training area for the Dambuster raids on Germany. Farmers complained that the practice bombing disturbed their horses, and one was very annoyed when his diesel tank on the tractor was hit by bullets.

North Sea Camp was founded in 1935 by the Borstal authorities for young offenders. It is situated out on Freiston shore. Thirty two boys and three officers walked from Stafford staying at village halls en route. They lived under canvas until the accommodation was built. They then set about reclaiming 600 acres of salt marsh by constructing dykes and a sea bank. So was established the thriving farm which exists today. In 1988 this became an adult open prison. The long distance footpath from Boston to Skegness passes the camp and the Freiston length of the sea bank is still maintained by the prison authority.

Freiston Hall Field Centre at the other end of the village, was opened in 1972 by the Local Education Authority. Its aim is to promote the teaching of the field sciences, such as geography, biology, geology and environmental studies by encouraging first hand investigations in the field. The Hall itself was built about 1800 but was extended and refurbished in 1920, and a new extension was completed in 1977.

Freiston village is a closely knit community with a wealth of activities for the socially inclined. The local community hall, named 'The Danny Flear Centre' in memory of a former benefactor of the village, is in constant use for a great variety of clubs and societies. The village boasts its own post office and a thriving butcher's shop where the local people meet and exchange news. Freiston is still surrounded by acres of prime agricultural land.

Friskney

Friskney is a large and widely scattered coastal parish some 13 miles north of Boston and eight miles south of Skegness. It borders upon the Wash and is situated between the marsh and the fens.

It is an ancient village and has not always been by the sea, for at low tide the remains of a prehistoric forest can be plainly seen. The remains of a Stone Age camp have also been found.

Of the Roman times there are several remains. The old sea bank is still known as the Roman Bank and about a mile behind it is High Street, locally known as Middle Street. It runs through fields and part of it is still a footpath. Behind the sea bank traces of the Roman salt pans can still be seen. It is probable that the Burgh Road was of Roman origin: it runs in an almost straight line for eight miles. In 1813, some half mile north-east of the church, the remains of a Roman aqueduct were discovered.

At some time following the Roman withdrawal the first church, dedicated to St Katherine of Alexandria, was built at Abbey Hills. It lasted through the Danish occupation, when Friskney was a southernmost part of the Danelaw.

Then came the Normans and Friskney passed to the de Kyme family. To them we probably owe the first church of All Saints on its present site. It was begun in 1135 and by the fragments that remain it must have been a magnificent edifice.

Friskney's lot during the Civil War was not an enviable one – Cromwell's forces held Boston while Wainfleet was for the King and Friskney had to help both sides in money and kind as well as sending men to fight and guard Wainfleet's 'Salem Bridge'.

Since the 14th century efforts had been made to drain the land, for much of the parish was under water for six months of the year. This was bitterly opposed by the inhabitants. In 1809, by a special Act of Parliament, drainage at last began and Friskney quickly changed. It was divided into 16 districts, 15 of which are still postal addresses.

In the days before the land was drained, wildfowling in the five decoys and along the coast was one of the main sources of livelihood. As many as 30,000 head of ducks and geese were sent to market annually. On the higher ground cranberries grew as many as 5,000 picks a year, which sold at 5/- per pick. Fishing was extensively carried on and later, when the railway came, large quantities of cockles and shrimps were gathered and sent to market. Later, as the land reclamation went on, potatoes were the main crop. These were sent by rail to the London and Yorkshire markets. During the latter part of this century market gardening has come into its own and large lorries, some of which go as far afield as Europe, now transport fresh vegetables.

Gone are the mills and the millers and the brickyard with its tall chimney. The blacksmiths remain but the horses they once shod have practically disappeared, though each year they pull the decorated drays on Chapel Feast Day. Two shops, two post offices and two pubs are still part of village life. There are no fishermen, land reclamation has taken over the fishing grounds.

Until the 19th century, Friskney had a mayor, appointed annually to see that law and order was kept and that the roads and dykes were in good order. Friskney today has upwards of 30 miles of roads.

Friskney is very fortunate in its beautiful church of All Saints. The lower part of the tower, transitional Norman 1137, is all that is left of the original building after a fire, then it passes through Early English and Perpendicular stages. It houses six bells and a clock and is entered by a magnificent arch. The foundation stone of the present building was laid in 1247. The nave is very high and the clerestory, on which are the remains of wall paintings, was added in the 14th century. The old roof, together with a chancel screen and two chantry screens have been well preserved.

Until the old school was built by public subscription in 1815, children were taught in a gallery in the church. In 1856, the joint salary of the schoolmaster and his wife was £52, paid from the charities for the education of poor children. In 1860 the present school was built and like its predecessor it is a Church school.

In 1650-1660 Friskney had its own witch, one Joane Clarke. She was committed to prison in Boston, on a charge of witchcraft. Soldiers had been called in to catch her, for which the parish had to pay £3.

Obbin Sylvester, a native, carved the beautiful bosses for the aisles of St Botolph's at Boston and Sir Walter Friskney, a judge at the Court of the Exchequer in the reigns of Edward III and Richard II gave the church its two aisles, the top part of the tower and the clerestory.

Alfred Tennyson was a frequent visitor to the vicarage in the early 1800s. It is said that the Lincolnshire dialect of their gardener was the inspiration for his poem *The Northern Farmer.*

Frithville ⁊⁊

Two hundred and fifty years ago the parish of Frithville was unenclosed marshland on the edge of the West Fen. In the 13th century monks from Kirkstead Abbey grazed their immense flocks of sheep on 500 acres of the Frith. There were no roads except a droveway from Sibsey into the marsh passing Swincotes, where probably a few people lived on the slightly higher ground. The graziers of Sibsey also had sheep on the marsh. In the summer the Frith would be white with the number of sheep, looked after by the scattered population. In the winter, when the marsh became swamp, the inhabitants made their living by fishing and wildfowling. They were an independent race, accepting strangers with strong reservations and resisting change.

The marsh was intersected by natural watercourses; one of these was called the Medlam and carried water from the higher ground at Revesby. It joined another waterway at the Frith, the Whistler, which entered the Witham at Antons Gowt. These waterways were used for transport by the local inhabitants.

Several attempts had been made to drain the marsh and nearby fen-lands, but were unsuccessful until the 19th century, when corn was needed to feed the army horses in the Napoleonic Wars. Eyes were again turned to the fens and marshes of Lincolnshire and the possibilities of renewing attempts to drain them. Sir Joseph Banks was an important promoter of the project. Parliament passed the necessary Acts and, in spite of the local people's objections, the work went ahead. The Frith became intersected by man-made drains. The Medlam was straightened and joined a new one, known as the West Fen Drain near Swincotes. One side of the new drain, which cuts the village into two parts, is now lined by trees planted to mark the Silver Jubilee of George V and the Coronation of George VI.

Roads were built on the banks of the waterways – straight and exposed to all the winds which blew. Beautiful brick bridges were constructed, high enough for the packet boats to pass underneath on their way to Boston market with the produce grown on the now fertile land. The men who had been fen slodgers became agricultural labourers working for yeoman farmers who owned their small farms.

Frith became Frithville, population 162, a village with a windmill, owned by Mr Tom Parker, to grind corn for making bread and animal foodstuffs which were delivered locally by horse and cart; his grandson

Derek now has a corn drier and lorries which deliver animal feed to a greater area. There was also a blacksmith's shop where horses were shod and implements mended; this is now owned by the blacksmith's grandson, Malcolm Sargeant, who has converted it into a service garage. One of the original public houses, The Ship, is now closed but there is still the White Hart where Parish Council meetings were once held; it is owned by Mrs M. Hobbs whose family came here in 1887. Mr Robert Crawford, whose father was once a blacksmith, now owns a large agricultural engineering firm with a Royal Warrant to supply equipment to the Queen's estates. One of the earlier farmer's grandsons, David Grant, employs local people in his vegetable packing station.

Under the Enclosure Act a fund was created for the building and maintenance of fen chapels – Frithville's was built in 1821 and dedicated to St Peter. The first burial in the churchyard was on 11th May 1823 and the first baptism administered in the same year. There was also a small church built off Fishtoft Drove which is now in the parish of Frithville. It was in the care of a curate living in the village but when there ceased to be a curate in the parish this little church was closed. In 1899 a Methodist chapel was built. The congregations of St Peter's and the chapel have joined an ecumenical partnership.

The school, which was built in the 1880s, once had 120 pupils but now takes juniors and infants only: a playgroup meets once a week in one of the classrooms.

At the turn of the century a reading room was erected where villagers could go to read the daily and local newspapers. The reading room became the village hall, and has been extended and modernised.

On the very fertile soil developed from the drained marshes many different crops are grown including corn, potatoes, sugar beet, brassicas and strawberries. Some farmers grow two crops a year on the same field – early potatoes followed by brassicas.

After the Second World War it was decided that Frithville was not to be developed and so it has, to a large extent, remained a close-knit community preserving the characteristics of the former fen men. Some neighbours have lived next door to each other in harmony for over 60 years. Many of the inhabitants were born and bred in the village – if you went to school together your age is not a secret – if you have an illness or bereavement the population supports the family – there is a sense of belonging.

Although Frithville is not a picturesque village attracting tourists its people do enjoy magnificent cloudscapes, beautiful sunsets and clear starlit nights. In summer it is a land of plenty: in winter, when the flat fields stretch under an overcast sky to the horizon, and the lonely cry of the peewit is heard at dusk, you may well have the feeling that the days when all was marsh are not so very far away.

Fulstow

Fulstow – 'Fugelstow' – is mentioned in the Domesday Book and is said to mean the home of a hermit. The village is eight miles north of Louth and is a pleasant place of approximately 550 population.

The church was built in the 13th century and dedicated to St Lawrence. In the porch are the carved stone effigies of Sir Robert de Hilton and his lady. The churchyard is combined with the manor gardens and beautifully kept.

In a field near the church is a mound. This is said by some to be a mass grave for 118 villagers who died of 'the sweating sickness'. Another theory is that the graves contain cattle struck down by a plague.

Until 1969 there were two pubs in the village, the Lord Nelson and the Cross Keys, but only the latter remains. Mr Cyril Brown is the publican and is the third generation of his family to be the landlord of this establishment.

The post office and general store, still a thriving business, is a lively meeting place for villagers.

Fulstow Hall has been the home of the Carlbom family since 1920. Mr Anthony Carlbom is the Swedish and Finnish consul in Grimsby. The Hall stands in very pleasant wooded grounds.

There used to be three chapels in the village but now only one remains, this being a Methodist chapel. The original building belonged to the Primitive Methodists.

Farming is the main occupation in the village, predominantly cereals, potatoes and beef cattle. There is also a large egg producing farm and a well known Lincolnshire turkey supplier.

A long established family, Maddison Bros, are well known for their expertise and knowledge of traction engines. Not far away lives Mr P. Clark, a railway enthusiast who has a collection of steam trains that he has restored and which can often be seen steaming up and down the track laid on his land.

The village has grown considerably since 1970 with two estates being built with several pleasing properties.

Gedney 🦢

In the Domesday Book Gedney was called Gadenai, taking its name from the enclosure of spikes which in Anglo-Saxon times was used to protect the island on which the church stands from roving bands coming into the Wash from the mainland of Europe. The sea in those times was so near that the island was surrounded at each high tide.

About the time of the Norman Conquest, Gedney had a Goose Fair – geese, sheep and donkeys were plentiful in the district. From the 12th century onwards large areas were drained, reclaimed and turned into rich arable land.

Seawards, beyond the last enclosure, the foreshore is now used by the Royal Air Force as a practice bombing range. In 1883 the Gedney Common Enclosure bank of 1874 gave way and the whole marsh was flooded to several feet. Before the advent of the car, Bank Holiday trips to the sea marsh by horse and wagon were popular; the great attractions being the roundabouts, swings and stalls selling mussels, cockles and samphire all collected off the marsh. Local people still gather the samphire which when cooked and pickled is eaten with cold meat.

The main feature of Gedney is certainly the church, known locally as the 'Cathedral of the Fens', a lovely stone building of Early English, Late Decorated and Perpendicular styles. It has a tower containing six bells and surmounted by a short octagonal spire.

The fine west door is 14th century and has a Latin inscription which translated says 'The peace of Christ be on this house and all dwelling in it – Here is our rest'. The wicket door has a small ivory Crucifixion scene on it and inside on the double bronze lock made by John Pett in the 14th century there is an inscription in Latin 'Beware Before Ayeset'.

A line round the tower shows where building was stopped during the Black Death and then continued with a different design afterwards. Stained glass is not a feature of Gedney church, a lot was lost when a land mine dropped nearby during the Second World War, but there is one outstanding example – the 14th century Jesse window which is similar to that in Chartres Cathedral in France.

The remains of an underground passage is thought to have led from the church to Abbot's Manor which stood nearby – the foundations of which with some coins, bones and stone coffins have been found.

The railway lines to Peterborough, Kings Lynn and Bourne were opened after permission was granted for use of the existing bridge at Sutton Bridge. The line was extended, later becoming the London, Midland and Scottish Railway. The line was largely used by farmers to send their produce to the large towns. The railway was finally closed after the Beeching cuts in 1965. In the late 1930s a vicar of Gedney was killed by a train whilst walking down the line.

In the parish register there are some strange names, ie in 1714 a woman called Jeflet Banishment Endurance entered bonds of matrimony – 20 years later her death was recorded. At that time there was a notion that should a woman marry without worldly possessions her previous debts could not be recorded – Susan Farran showed her penniless state by coming to Gedney church for her wedding to David Wilkinson dressed only in a sheet with a hole cut for her head.

In 1900 Edward Bell who lived in Gedney Fen was hanged in Lincoln Prison – he had poisoned his wife with strychnine. In 1860 William Pepper was sentenced to death for sheep stealing.

In 1982 the village was visited by over 400 people whose surname was Gedney, Gadney or Gidney. They travelled from Canada, America, Australia and many parts of Great Britain to meet and take part in a special service in Gedney church. The postmaster had been given special dispensation for letters and cards to be franked in Gedney.

Gipsey Bridge

This nucleus of houses in the parish of Thornton le Fen is grouped where the road from Frithville carries the main traffic around Boston to Langrick. It is a predominantly agricultural area with ribbon development housing on the Coningsby road.

Since the 1960s three new housing estates have been built to enlarge the village. In 1987 the once abandoned public house The Windmill was reopened. There is a shop-cum-post office and a county primary school taking 50 children at present. A Methodist chapel stands at the roadside and a few meetings are held in its school room.

No one has the real story about the name Gipsey, but the bridge over the stream, which is now the Castledyke Drain, gives its name to the village. One theory is that gipsey means 'wandering', so it is the 'bridge over the wandering stream'.

Gosberton

Six miles from Spalding, at the A16 and A152 road junction, the village is overlooked by the parish church of St Peter and St Paul. Viewed from any direction it is a rather pleasing sight. Certainly from the Boston and Eaudike roads at sundown one can see the tall steeple majestically rising from surrounding trees in sharp silhouette against a crimson sky – a fine example of the lovely sunsets the fenlands of Lincolnshire can be proud of.

The present spelling was established in the 1500s but in the Domesday Book both 'Gozeberdecca' and 'Gosberkirk' are recorded. It is a compact village from which straggling roads reach out to various hamlets embraced within the parish – Belnie, Westhorpe, Rigbolt, Cheal, Clough and Risegate. All are steeped in history with Saxon, Danish and Roman influences and indicative that Gosberton rose from the marshes.

Gosberton Bank is a reminder of the Romans' foresight to avoid encroachment by the sea. From here, on a clear day, as many as a dozen different churches can be counted. Nearby Risegate Eau, Hammond Beck and Forty Foot drains are evidence of the hard work involved to rid the area of waterlogging and achieve its present fertile state.

Roads like Wargate Way are reminders of past history when in the 1300s much land around the church was owned by the La Warre family. Two houses now modernised, Rigbolt and Monks Hall, have past connections with monastic orders and rumour, still unproved, has it that underground passages connect these to the church. Cressy Hall, the third on its site, once boasted a huge heronry recorded to have had no less than 80 nests in one tree! The grandeur of Cressy and its chapel has now gone but the imposing red bricked house makes a beautiful springtime picture, its old moat and surrounding field amass with golden daffodils.

Springtime in Gosberton is indeed pleasant – many by-roads are planted with flowering bulbs and most gardens offer a colourful display. The little hall behind the church is a hive of industry providing homemade fare and cups of tea to countless visitors from near and far who journey to see the bulbfields, Spalding Flower Parade and many decorated churches and chapels. Gosberton's three denominations all put tremendous effort into the lovely arrangements, certainly worthy of a visit.

The church of St Peter and St Paul, the Baptist and the Methodist chapels are the only three remaining buildings providing for spiritual needs whereas for those in need of refreshment there are two – The Bell and Five Bells. Once there were six or seven of each! The two inns also offer excellent bar and restaurant meals. The number of shops has diminished over past decades but bakery, butchery, grocery and green-grocery provisions are amply available with post office, clothing, furniture, hardware and antiques shops also. Two banks open twice weekly. One, Barclays, was once the council pound, latterly for storage of tools but formerly to impound stray cattle.

Electricity is now the main source of power but in 1856 the gas house was built for £1,500 and the local gaslighter made his nightly round of 20 lights. The coke by-product was sold for 3d per bag regardless of size so it was beneficial to send the strongest member of the family for supplies!

The public hall was built in 1872 for £1,000 by public subscription on ground donated by Lord Brownlow. Behind this is a well kept bowling green and flourishing snooker and billiards club.

Gosberton House until recently educated children of lesser learning abilities and, although they are still taught within the grounds, the house itself is soon to be a private rest home for the elderly. Another such facility is the council owned Bank House where 40 residents are looked after and entertained by caring staff.

Snowhill on the A16 junction, once the site of a workhouse, is supposedly so called because nearby cottages were all whitewashed – now long gone. The village today has a motley array of buildings but nevertheless, once settled Gosberton residents are usually loathe to leave. For some, however, 'Fame is The Spur' – Sir George Bolles of Cawood Hall and Sir Thomas Boor Crosby of the Eaudike each became Lord Mayor of London in 1617 and 1912 respectively.

Grainthorpe 🐑

Grainthorpe is a pleasant village mid-way between Grimsby and Mablethorpe on the coast road. Its present population is about 650, and considering the number of new houses springing up all over the village, that number will soon increase. Known as 'Germundtorp' in the

St Clement's Church, Grainthorpe

Domesday Book, Grainthorpe can trace its history back to Roman times, when the salt works in the northern marsh were at Grainthorpe and Marshchapel. A Roman road runs from Lincoln through Claybridge, Sixhills, Ludford and Tows along Pear Tree Lane to the coast near Beacon Hill at Grainthorpe.

The most significant building is the church, which dates back to the early 14th century, with a tower of a slightly later date. In the chancel is a very fine (but damaged) brass, with a foliated cross, probably in memory of Stephen-le-See, vicar of the church of 'Germethorp' during the 14th century. Next to the church is a fine old farmhouse with a tithe barn. Another listed building is the beautiful Georgian Grainthorpe Hall, now a thriving smorgasbord restaurant. The village also boasts a very old cottage, at Poors' End. A similar 'mud and stud' cottage was dismantled recently and is being stored until a suitable site is found.

Farming is still the main industry in the area. There are dairy and arable farms, ranging from the small family farm to giant concerns. Down Ivy Lane is a large turkey farm. With the decline in jobs in farming, many other businesses have also sprung up. The old wheelwright's is now a horticultural nursery, there is a motor workshop, a garage, two hairdressers, painters and decorators, two builders, a plumber, an artist and an accountant. Down Fen Lane is a fruit and vegetable wholesale business.

The village shop and post office has also moved with the times – formerly Sowbys' Stores, it is now a busy modern shop. There are boarding kennels down Biergate and the old mill is still standing, though now without its sails. The Black Horse is the only pub in the village now, where there once were four. The last to close was the Bricklayers' Arms, converted to a house in the 1970s. Several mobile services also come to the village – chiropodist, video shop, library, butcher, baker, wet fish, and the fish and chip van.

Grainthorpe County primary school dates back to 1851, when it was established by a legacy from one John Lill, a most generous benefactor who also endowed the village with land to be cultivated by the poor – these allotments are still going strong. The school is now thriving, thanks to the new houses bringing new families to the village.

Grainthorpe has an excellent playing field, maintained by the village. It is used for cricket and football matches, and has a well-equipped playground for the younger children, with swings and slides.

In addition to the church, there is a very active Methodist chapel and Sunday school, one of the oldest chapels in the Louth Circuit. Years ago, there were three different types of Methodist chapel here, but now only one remains.

Last but not least are facilities for the elderly in Grainthorpe. There are 14 sheltered bungalows in Mill Garth, with a resident warden. As well as various social events held in their lounge, there is a Welcome Club held once a fortnight for all the pensioners in the village.

The neighbouring hamlet of Conisholme has a very old church, which contains an interesting ancient sun stone, with pagan and Christian symbols. There is an active Methodist chapel here, a garden nursery and the old Conisholme Village Institute, which has been restored by the East Lindsey Marsh Villages Society. Applebys, one of the most successful businesses in the area, is based at Conisholme. Here they have their famous ice cream shop and tea room, and here too is the office for the famous coach company.

Grainthorpe often passes unnoticed, as the main road slips along the side of the village. We hope that now you may wish to take a closer look.

Great Gonerby

The village of Great Gonerby is one of the oldest in the Grantham area and was one of the villages owned by the Belton House estate. The farms were owned and the farm labourers were employed by the Brownlows.

The early settlement was a little out of the actual site of the village and there are remains of a Roman camp in the Ridge area.

Later camps were set up by Cromwell in the 17th century and he himself lodged in a house in Pond Street locally known as 'Cromwell's Cottage'. Here he must have planned his attack on Grantham, as the village stands 300 ft above the town.

The church stands on the site of an ancient Saxon place of worship and has an interesting stone alcove and other Tudor effigies and carvings. The clock has been the target of the 'clock pelters', who pelted the face with either stones or clods of earth to try to stop the clock so that no one knew the time and the workers would go home earlier – whether it really worked for or against them is difficult to know!

The hill down into Grantham has been lowered by ten to 15 ft but it is still quite steep and when it was the Great North Road, which took all traffic through the village, one can imagine the difficulties of the stage coaches and the ease with which highwaymen were able to hold up and rob the travellers. There were teams of heavy horses to haul up the stage coaches and in inclement weather it was often impossible to make the journey through.

The houses in the Main Street are mostly Georgian, although several are much earlier, and built of Ancaster stone. There were several inns but now only one remains, the others converted into private houses or pulled down. One in particular in Green Street was early 18th century and is now a house known as Sutton Lodge. Also in Green Street was a side road called The Wong and this was used to gather the livestock before sending them to Grantham market. The name has been removed within the last few years and it is now part of Green Street.

Continuing round into Pond Street one comes first to Spring End, which indicates that there were, and still are, springs, which led into the pond at the end of the street, sadly now concreted over and something of an eyesore. Opposite Pond Street is Long Street in which the Old Manor is still standing and occupied, also the coach house and other old cottages probably belonging to the manor at one time.

At the other end of the village leading into the A1, which bypasses the village, was a battlefield in the Civil War. Bones and other indications were found in the excavations when the Little Chef was built.

Wesley preached in the village but the house in which he lived was sadly pulled down so no one knows the exact place. There are still several farms in the village and it is still a rural community, but much land has been sold for building and the village is rapidly getting larger.

Great Ponton 🎻

Great Ponton is a pleasant village largely nestled between the A1 and the waters of the Cringle brook and the river Witham.

It is said to be the 'Ad Pontem' of the Romans. Ermine Street to the east of the village, numerous finds relating to the Roman period and the discovery of a mosaic pavement in a field to the north of the present school, bear testimony to the presence of those foreign invaders of long ago.

The East Coast main railway line to Scotland runs through the eastern part of the parish, though the once thriving railway station has been closed for some 30 years, the nearest now being at Grantham, four miles away.

Facilities in the village include a post office/shop, village hall, playing field, church, public house, petrol filling station and primary school.

The church of the Holy Cross stands in an elevated position in the village. It is dominated by a splendid and lofty tower built as late as 1519 by Anthony Ellys, a wool merchant of the Staple of Calais who lived in his manor house adjacent to the church. It is a fine example of Perpendicular style. On the three outer faces is the legend 'Thynke and Thanke God of All'. The tower was Anthony Ellys's thank-offering for preservation and material success. Travelling abroad must have been dangerous in those days, particularly for someone carrying money, and one story tells of barrels of Calais sand being delivered to the manor house. Hidden in the sand was gold secreted there by the wool merchant!

His manor house became the rectory in 1921 but ceased to be so in 1984. It has since been sold and is now a private dwelling house. It has considerable style and distinction, being built of local limestone and with stone mullioned windows. It dates back to about 1500.

The fiddle weather-vane on the church tower is believed to be unique in England. Legend has it, though no one can vouch for the truth of it, that many years ago a fiddler used to visit Great Ponton to entertain the villagers. When he announced his intention of going to America the villagers paid his fare. In America he made his fortune and when he returned he had the weather-vane erected. The fiddle is attached to one of the eight crocketed pinnacles of the tower. It is said that it revolves on an old ginger-beer bottle marble. After it blew down in 1978 and had to be refixed, it was found to be weathered to the thinness of brown paper!

The Archer Endowed Church of England school was founded in 1717 by a wealthy landowner, William Archer, and endowed by him with two cottages and some land. That trust is still in being at the present time. Money from it has helped many youngsters from the village in the purchase of tools or books needed for their further education. A second school in the same grounds was opened in 1875. Sadly, both schools, together with the school house, had to be demolished in 1960 to make way for the A1 dual carriageway. A new primary school was opened in January of that year.

The 1960s brought changes to other parts of the village too. During that decade many of the old stone cottages were pulled down to be replaced by both council and private housing. However, enough of the old buildings remain to enable Great Ponton to retain its attractive appearance.

Across the fields from the main village and standing by the river is Mill Farm. It has an attached room housing the water-wheel, which in days long gone drove the machinery which ground the local farmers' corn. Although the wheel is still there much restoration will be needed if it is ever to be set in motion again.

That is Great Ponton, a village great in name but not in population. This has steadily declined since the beginning of the 20th century and is now less than 300. Most of the old trades and businesses have disappeared (there were once wheelwrights, coal merchants, bakers, grocers and even a shoe-maker in the village). However, a blacksmith's trade is still being carried on in a building which has been used for that purpose for almost 100 years.

Hagworthingham

Hagworthingham is a fair sized village, with narrow twisting lanes, and is reached on the A158 (Skegness) road midway between Spilsby and Horncastle. There are just over 200 souls, most of them being 'incomers' who have chosen to live in the village. There are still a few of the original properties, although much new building has been erected.

It is sometimes called Hag, which is a pity because such a pretty place does not deserve an ugly name.

It is close to the site of the battle of Winceby (October 1643) and to

69

Snipedales Nature Reserve and Country Park, developed by the Lincolnshire & South Humberside Trust for Nature Conservation.

The Old Hall on the Main Road is an 18th century house, still used as a residence. The New Hall on the corner of Church Lane is a Georgian private residence, nicely restored and maintained.

Stockwith Mill is no longer used for its original purpose and was mentioned by Tennyson in his poem, *The Brook*. The buildings, which are 18th century, are used as a restaurant and craft shop.

There were once three churches, two Methodists and one Church of England. One was demolished in the 1970s and the other converted to a residence. Holy Trinity remains. There is evidence of 12th, 13th and 15th century work on this church and until the 1970s it had a peal of eight bells. Sadly the bells were sold to Welbourn (Lincoln) to raise money for the repair to the tower which collapsed in 1972. The church-yard overlooks a valley in the beautiful Wolds and a barrow believed to be a very old burial mound can be seen on the way to Lusby a mile away through the beck, which has a footbridge.

Hagworthingham windmill is now capped and is a reminder of the milling and merchant business of the Ellis family. The village pump has been restored in Manor Road.

There are many attractions in this delightful area and Hagworthingham remains one of the unspoiled villages of the Wolds.

Harmston 🐿️

Harmston is situated just off the A607 Lincoln to Grantham road, about five miles south of Lincoln and one mile from Waddington, the well known RAF base.

The village (approximately 430 inhabitants), situated in the Viking Way and built on the Cliff edge, has fine views of the Witham vale and of Lincoln Cathedral. There are many stone cottages and farmhouses, a post office and one public house, The Thorold Arms.

The church, built of stone, is dedicated to All Saints. The incumbent is the Rev R. Bell, living in the vicarage, and he is also the rector of Coleby, a neighbouring village. The church has a Norman tower; the chancel and nave were rebuilt in 1868. In the church is a small Saxon cross carved with a Crucifixion and a Resurrection, which was discovered in the walls of the old manor house. There is a peal of eight bells and fine monuments to the Thorold family, who built Harmston Hall in

1456. One is to Sir George Thorold, Lord Mayor of London in 1720. Another is a brass inscription to Margaret Thorold who died in 1616, mother of 19 children.

The present Hall was built for Sir Charles Thorold in the early 18th century. This fine stone mansion has been part of a hospital complex for the mentally handicapped for the past 50 years. Because of changes in hospital care, the Hall, buildings and grounds are now for sale.

The National school, a stone building in the centre of the village, was closed in the early 1980s. It reopened in 1989 as a youth residential centre for Christian groups of children and adults, renamed The Cliff Centre.

The Memorial Hall on School Lane was built by Major Cockburn of Harmston Hall after the First World War. It is regularly used for social functions and meetings.

In days gone by the village was renowned for staging one of the finest one day agricultural shows in the country. The venue for the show was the beautiful grounds of Harmston Hall and it was at this show in 1904 that the NFU was born. A group of farmers at the show were discussing the problems of the day and decided to hold a meeting for farmers at the Albion Hotel (Lincoln) two days later. The Lincolnshire Farmers Union was formed and four years later it became the National Farmers Union.

Heckington

The village is recorded in the Domesday survey as Echintune and was then held of the Crown by Gilbert de Gaunt. In the reign of James I, Henry, the ninth Lord Cobham of Heckington, and his brother George were convicted of high treason; the latter was beheaded and Lord Cobham was spared, only to live in poverty until his death in 1619.

There was a church here in 1086, but the present St Andrew's church is at least the third building to stand on the same site and is considered by many to be one of the finest parish churches of the Decorated period. Richard de Pottesgrave who was rector in the early 14th century built the chancel, probably with financial help from King Edward II, to whom he was Chaplain and Confessor. This rector's tomb is on the north side of the chancel, as is the Easter Sepulchre which is one of the three finest examples in England.

Adjacent to Heckington station is the last surviving eight-sailed windmill in England. The mill stopped working under sail in 1942, and was acquired by the County Council in 1953. After restoration it is now grinding again at weekends. The windmill is open to the public as is the nearby Craft and Heritage Centre, which is still known as the Pearoom because, before its restoration by Heckington Village Trust, the building was owned by a well-known seed firm and local people worked there sorting peas.

In 1888 four almshouses were erected near the village green with a legacy from Henry Godson, and in 1905 four more were built near the church by the generosity of Edward Godson. Following the Charity Commissioners' new scheme for all the village charities established in 1974, all the almshouses were modernised. The income from the remaining charities is distributed annually.

A new primary school was opened in 1987 and the old premises are leased to the Parochial Church Council and used by all the uniformed youth organisations and the Youth Club.

It is claimed that Dick Turpin slept at The Nag's Head, an inn near the village green. This may well be the case, as at his trial in York, Turpin was convicted of stealing a mare and foal from Heckington common. After a second trial for stealing another horse from the same owner he was sentenced and executed a month later, on the 7th April 1739.

Samuel Jessup (born 1752), a wealthy grazier of Heckington, consumed 226,934 pills and drank 40,000 bottles of medicine over the years before he died at the age of 65!

In 1811 the first English aeronaut, Mr James Sadler, flew his hydrogen balloon at a record average speed of 84 mph in a gale between Birmingham and Heckington. Sadler fell out whilst attempting to land but his co-pilot Burcham continued until he encountered an ash tree.

William Little who lived at Heckington Hall patented a sheep dip in the early 1870s. Known as Little's Dip, it was still being used within living memory. It is in the Hall grounds that Heckington and District Agricultural Society's Annual Show has been held since 1867. Now held as a two day event on the last weekend in July, record crowds attend and for many Heckingtonians it is still a celebration of the Feast, with stuffed chine and plum bread on the menu.

Heckington no longer claims its former title of Queen of Villages, but did win the Best Kept Village Competition in 1974 and again in 1985. The village used to straddle the A17 which over the years carried an increasing volume of heavy traffic. After a long period of campaigning by the Parish Council and concerted pressure from the Bypass Group a new bypass was opened in December 1982 and the road through the village is now the B1394.

Now the traffic in the village is increasing as new estates are being built, and with its status as a Key Village, Heckington's present population of 2,000 will rise dramatically as some 500 new houses are expected to be built over the next few years.

Heighington

Heighington lies four miles south-east of Lincoln. A beck runs from the Old Mill through the centre of the village where there are some fine stone houses. It has a unique chapel of ease with schoolroom adjoining, the tower being 13th century, and a Victorian Methodist chapel close by.

Heighington boasts two public houses, a post office, supermarket, newsagent, modern primary school, two village halls and a sports field.

The village is now suffering from excessive development due to it being designated a Lincoln 'Main Village'.

Hemswell

A quiet charming village with a population of 250, nestling at the foot of the limestone ridge, halfway between Lincoln and Scunthorpe.

It was originally called Elmswell and was a part of the Aslacoe Wapentake; in the Lindsey Division of Lincolnshire. It is now in North Lincolnshire since the formation of the County of Humberside.

Hemswell has expanded very little over the years and old properties have been sympathetically restored so that the use of limestone is still very much in evidence.

Several interesting features are maintained. The chalybeate springs, once the main source of drinking water for the villagers (and which probably explain the name of the village) still run out of the hillside. Piped water came to the village in 1948.

The pinfold, once a pound for stray cattle, was a small square of neglected ground until 1977 when the Parish Council had a stone wall built round it. A seat was installed and the Women's Institute and the

Evergreen Club planted four shrubs there to commemorate the Queen's Silver Jubilee.

A maypole has been maintained here since the days when May Day was one of the highlights of the village calendar. Since it was refurbished in Jubilee year, maypole dancing has become an annual event once more. New braids were bought and costumes made for a team of twelve dancers. The boys' smocks are embroidered with the traditional patterns and the girls wear long petticoats and skirts and fen bridle style bonnets. It has become almost a tradition for the Lincoln Morris Men to attend this May Day Bank Holiday celebration, when everyone has the opportunity to dance round the maypole.

The school and adjoining school house was built in 1859 for 70 children at a cost of £560, defrayed by Sir Thomas Whichcote, Bart. It eventually closed in 1970 and in 1974 the school became a village hall and the school house a private residence.

The shop and post office is a valuable asset to village life. Both Wesleyan and Methodist chapels closed many years ago but 13th cen-

Willow Cottage, Hemswell

74

tury All Saints' church, recently the subject of extensive restoration work, looks set to enjoy an active future.

The character of the village has changed significantly over the past 40 years. Smallholdings have been absorbed into bigger farms and there are few signs now that this is an agricultural area. Apart from a small wrought iron industry and a small builder's it is now mainly a residential conservation area.

RAF Hemswell was among the famous bomber stations of Lincolnshire during the Second World War, but is now being developed as a separate parish situated on the Cliff two miles from the village.

Hemswell's 'twin' village, Harpswell, is just the distance of a field away and is mainly a farming community spread beside the main road to the coast, the A631. It is overlooked by St Chad's church, which is proudly maintained by the small community and shares a vicar with Hemswell and Glentworth.

A new feature is a garden nursery now using some of the land being taken out of crop production.

Holdingham

One mile to the north of Sleaford is the hamlet of Holdingham (formerly spelled Haldingham). It is not mentioned in the Domesday Book, but was probably included in the manor of Sleaford.

There was once a chapel at Holdingham, dedicated to St Mary the Virgin, but this has long since disappeared.

Holdingham is noted for being the presumed birthplace of Richard-de-Haldingham. Originally a cleric in the diocese of Lincoln, he was made a Canon of Hereford in 1299. While there he produced the 'Mappa Mundi'. Now in Hereford Cathedral, this is one of the earliest maps in England. It represents the world as an island, surrounded by ocean, with Jerusalem as its centre.

The Jolly Scotchman public house was redecorated by the brewery in the mid 1950s. Not realising the name had nothing to do with Scotland, they used Scotch plaid in the interior and men were represented doing the Highland Fling and playing the bagpipes in the two main stained glass windows. In fact it stands on the site of the old toll gatehouse and was so named after the keeper who used to 'scotch' the wheels of the carts while the owners went to pay their toll. The public house sign was altered some years ago and now shows the 'Jolly Scotchman'.

Holton Beckering

Holton Beckering lies in pleasant countryside some twelve miles north-east of Lincoln and about three miles north of the main road from Lincoln to Skegness as it passes through Wragby. Because it isn't on a main road it has not become a suburb of the City. It is still a country village – although it is more accurate to call it a hamlet: the population is under 100.

The great increase in mechanisation of farming since the Second World War has gradually led to fewer agricultural workers being needed to work the land, so, as in so many other villages, Holton is no longer occupied by people who get their living by working on the farms in the parish.

But there are still traces of old times to be seen. In Beckering (which in much earlier days was separate from, and more populous than, Holton) can still be seen some bumps and hollows in the ground that indicate a deserted medieval village. People digging in their gardens occasionally turn up pieces of old pottery or old clay pipes. Deep ploughing has destroyed most of the 'ridge and furrow' which was visible in many of the fields, although they can be seen and photographed from the air.

In the church and especially in the churchyard are other reminders, less of things than of some of the people who lived here. A memorial to one whose work was known and admired outside his birthplace is in the churchyard in front of the church; it is to John Espin. Together with his brother William and more famous brother Thomas he travelled around Lincolnshire making watercolour sketches of buildings and of architectural remains.

The other headstones in the churchyard are mostly memorials to villagers not known beyond their community. But in the north-east corner are buried two young airmen, a Canadian and a New Zealander, who perished during the Second World War. The 12 and 626 Squadrons of Bomber Command were stationed at Wickenby (but many of the RAF buildings were in Holton). On the airfield, near the boundary of Wickenby and Holton, is a memorial erected in 1981 to the 1,080 men who died on active service from the Wickenby base.

The memorials inside the church at Holton include some to people whose influence was wider than that of the other villagers. On the north wall is a tablet to the memory of Gilbert Caldecott who died in 1796.

He was a well-known figure in Lincoln, where he lived and owned property. He was Sheriff of the county in 1747. The Caldecotts came into the parish during the late 1590s, and gradually bought up nearly all Beckering and then Holton.

The Holton estate was sold in 1917, and the Hall was occupied by a succession of owners, until it was taken over by the Army as a convalescent home. In 1945 it was bought by a community of pacifists to house conscientious objectors who had been given land work as an alternative to military service. A few of them with their descendants still live in the village. The Hall is now in private ownership, but the 'big room' is used by the village for meetings, harvest suppers and the like – the old school being no longer usable.

Now at the end of the 20th century, little of the agricultural nature of the village is left – two farmers have retired and much of their land has been sold to neighbouring farmers and the farmhouses have new owners.

In contrast to the new residents in the village, two cottages have been occupied by the same families for many years. They were built towards the end of the 19th century for the wheelwright and the blacksmith. Wheelwright's Cottage has been in the occupation of one family only and one resident belongs to the fourth generation of that family. One resident of the Blacksmith's Cottage has lived there for some 60 years and was born in the village.

The oldest building in the village is, of course, the church of All Saints. Built some five or six centuries ago, it is a handsome building which in spite of restoration still has some of its original features. There are the two large shields carved on the stone wall on either side of the south porch, with the arms of Roos and de Bekering. The doorway, the little window in the west wall of the south aisle and west tower are all original, as is the south arcade. During the restorations of 1851 (by Nicholson) and 1859/60 and 1870/4 (by Sir G.G. Scott) the plain deal pews, pulpit and desk were swept away and a fine oak screen erected and oak pews. The reredos is beautiful; it was made at the time of this lavish restoration by an Italian craftsman who was an expert in gold mosaic work; the motifs of angels playing musical instruments are particularly interesting.

Holton le Moor 🌿

To see England at its best, the England that romantic poets write about, visit Holton le Moor on a spring morning and take a walk down the Gatehouse Lane, where fresh green leaves make a tunnel over one's head. Near a bend is the Woodman's white cottage, with its neat box-edged path and blossoming apple tree.

On the opposite side of the road is a glimpse of the Park, with cattle grazing under the trees and a red brick Georgian house, a listed building, which has been the home of the Dixon-Gibbons family since the 1780s. At one time the entire village was owned by the family. The houses they built have the unusual feature of name plaques. These names make an interesting study giving clues to the history of the village. At the same time it is possible to note various types of brickwork and bricks used in the construction and ornamentation of the houses.

This must also be the only village in Lincolnshire where pargetting decorates buildings and shows the history of Britain as well as of the village. Many people find much pleasure in tracing this, and fascinating details of some village characters too, on the village Moot Hall. The gable end of this is a copy of the well known Moot Hall at Aldeburgh.

Some pargetting appears on the nearby school including a list of names of the first pupils to be taught there. The school, with its colourful plaque of 'For God, King and Country' over its doors, is set in spacious playgrounds, including the March Yard, sheltered by belts of trees and carpeted with snowdrops in early spring. This pleasant, secluded area is open for public use and earned its name from the fact that the militia were trained there by the then High Sheriff.

Adjoining this is St Luke's churchyard, a paradise for the botanist and ornithologist, with its wide variety of plant life and different species of birds. The church has a turret which contains two bells, made from the original bell given by Nicholas Bestoe. This was broken when the tower was destroyed, but a rubbing was taken of the inscription, which is in the church. The name of Nicholas Bestoe, a wool merchant, is to be found on the list of Merchant Tailors in the Merchant Tailors' Hall in London. Unfortunately the Holton home of this family disappeared long ago, but plans and some details of the building remain and the name is retained in that of a house on the site.

Built in 1910 the Moot Hall is an interesting and attractive building.

The iron railings outside bear the slogan 'Holton will flourish if all do their share'. May it long continue to do so.

Huttoft

Huttoft, a very pleasant village on the East Coast, of Danish origin, lies between the villages of Mumby and Sutton-on-Sea. The population is approximately 480.

Access to the beach at Huttoft Bank is about three miles away, and can be reached via Jolly Common Lane or Sea Lane. Car parking, picnicking and caravaning facilities are to be found in this area.

The church of St Margaret dates back to the early 13th century, and the County primary school nearby was built in 1840. The Methodist chapel dates back to 1857. Services are held regularly at both places of worship. Other amenities to be found in the village are a petrol station and garage, a post office, shop, animal feeds mill, village hall and public house.

Activities in the village include a playgroup, Mothers and Toddlers group, Over 50s club, bingo, Youth Club and Women's Institute (founded in 1922).

There are numerous public footpaths in the area for those who enjoy walking in these beautiful surroundings.

Ingham

Ingham is a village of just under 700 inhabitants, nestling at the foot of the Lincoln Edge, eight miles north of Lincoln. There has been a settlement here since the time of the Saxons and Danes settling in England, as the ending of the name 'ham' indicates. In the Domesday Book, it is spelled Ingeham.

In the centre of the village is a spacious, picturesque, tree scattered village green. The village originally grew up around the green, a cluster of grey stone houses and cottages, added to later by the Victorians. However, as with most villages, it has now spread quite considerably.

There has been a church here since the 13th century, but the present church of All Saints was rebuilt about 1796, reportedly after a fire. It is a typical small village church, very well kept, and along with the churchyard has plenty to interest the historian. In front of the church-

Ingham Church

yard is a second small village green, until about 35 years ago the village pond, but now a tree-shaded oasis of peace, with a seat for quiet browsing.

The village is only three miles from Scampton RAF camp, where the Red Arrows are based, and from October to February we enjoy thrilling free shows as they rehearse their routines.

For the walker, there are a number of easy and interesting walks in the vicinity of the village, with a number of public footpaths. The Black Horse, built 300 years ago, and The Inn on the Green, built in the 19th century, are situated on the edge of the green and maintain their old world charm. The Inn on the Green is popular, whilst the Black Horse is a typical cosy village pub renowned as being a haunt of the Dambusters during the Second World War.

For caravanners there is a Caravan Club CL site just off the village green, well maintained and kept by very friendly and helpful people. Two shops, a post office, an off-licence and a doctor's surgery provide the necessities of life.

Ingham is a very lively village, with a modern village hall where invariably there is something happening, and the friendly villagers are always glad to welcome visitors to anything that is going on, whether in the village hall, at the Anglican and Methodist churches, or in the open air.

Keelby

There has been a settlement at Keelby since time immemorial, as artefacts excavated locally testify. Romans, Saxons and Normans all passed this way, Keelby being mentioned in the Domesday Book as Chelebi. The name, meaning 'ridge village', was given by the Danes.

The oldest buildings are a tiny medieval domestic chapel, now preserved as a shop selling elegant wrought ironware and other household goods, incorporated into Church Farm house; and the medieval church of St Bartholomew, inside which the earliest memorial is to John South, 1591. Another interesting memorial is to two sisters, Annie and Dorothy Lancaster, victims of the *Titanic* disaster. Outside, there is an ancient cross.

Keelby was originally an agricultural village. A century ago it was mainly a service village with many tradesmen, now it is a dormitory village with a population rapidly approaching 3,000.

The old part of Keelby, lying near the church and playing field, is quite distinct from the extensive new estates which almost surround it. Sadly, all the picturesque old thatched whitewashed cottages have been replaced by new housing, but near the church is a short row of five old cottages whose thick chalk walls have been raised in brick and re-roofed. The remaining older buildings are Georgian or Victorian, a few displaying their date of construction, as the Manor House, 1794.

John Wesley came through here on his way to Grimsby in the late 18th century and his influence is still evident.

To make life easier for those who are unwell or getting on in years, there are modern council bungalows, sheltered flats at Hubert Ward House, named after a popular village doctor, and a residential home at Walnut House, this same doctor's old home. Among several bequests, one by Mrs Alice South in 1605 still provides a small gift at Christmas for several retired villagers.

There is a small shopping centre with five shops – a supermarket, post office, bakery, newsagent-cum-greengrocer, and a DIY shop. A little further away is a 'chippie', haberdashery, hairdresser, sailing equipment supplier, another supermarket, a library open four days a week and a health centre. There are several haulage contractors, garages, a saw-mill and several farms, the village being surrounded by arable land. A certain amount of traffic congestion near the shops may soon necessitate one way streets.

Walking is easy, with access to Brocklesby, the Earl of Yarborough's estate village, Limber with its mausoleum, Roxton Woods, the springs which flow into Suddle Beck babbling gaily after a rainstorm, and several bridle paths. For fox hunting enthusiasts, the Earl of Yarborough's world famous hounds meet regularly in winter. Needless to say, horse riding is a popular activity here, though pasture is difficult to find.

Keelby village

82

A great beauty of this district is its wide open vistas, the vast skies and glorious sunsets. If you come to Keelby, take a walk down little Topper Lane, which is the truly country bit of the village. In winter, admire the snowdrops and aconites nearby and in spring, the beautiful pink and white cherry trees in Manor Street. For those who know where to look, it is easy to find wild flowers, foliage and even bay for flavouring the cooking, but, alas, no mushrooms nowadays.

Kettlethorpe & Torksey

The hamlets of Kettlethorpe, Laughterton and Fenton are situated eleven miles north-west of Lincoln (A57), bordered by the Roman Foss Dyke and A156 and the A1133 and the river Trent.

Kettlethorpe is famous for its connection with Lady Katherine Swynford, third wife of John of Gaunt, Duke of Lancaster, an ancestress of our present Royal Family by the Beaufort line. All that remains of her home, the property of her first husband Sir Hugh Swynford, is the old archway and part of the moat. The present Hall is a private residence, a pleasant 18th century house, and the church opposite is in a charming setting. It is mainly early 19th century, having been rebuilt and altered at various times.

Laughterton is on the A1133 and has caravan sites, a scout camp and a golf course. There is easy access to the river Trent via Marsh Lane and the area is very popular with anglers. The local inn is called The Friendship.

Fenton, the other corner of the triangle of villages, has an old maltings and the local inn, The Carpenter's Arms. The whole area is surrounded by arable land growing corn and root crops, and by chicken farms and pig farms.

Torksey, the neighbouring village, has many attractions. It is a village for boating (at Torksey Lock), fishing and golf, but has a past much more important than its size suggests today. It is situated on the A1133 Gainsborough road. Torksey is mentioned in the Domesday Book as a town, and before that was a focal point for the Roman defences, where the Foss Dyke joins the Trent.

Torksey Lock has a pleasant river bank walk. Pottery was found when the site known as Little London was excavated and it is known there were thriving potteries in the area. Torksey pottery can be seen at the Usher Gallery in Lincoln.

The village has a well-sited ruin known as Torksey Castle, built in the 16th century. It was sacked by the Royalists to rout the Cromwellians during the Civil War and was never rebuilt. The plain exterior of the village church belies its best work and atmosphere inside. There was also a mint during Roman and medieval times. The local inns are the Hume Arms and the White Swan at Torksey Lock. There is also a motel nearby on the A156.

Kirkby-cum-Osgodby

The administrative parish of Kirkby-cum-Osgodby is made up of four villages – Kirkby, Osgodby, Kingerby and Usselby.

Kingerby, once a larger community, is now a sparsely populated area reaching down to the river Ancholme at its western boundary. St Peter's church (13th century), now in the care of the Redundant Churches Fund, is, possibly, the third church on the site of what was once a Roman camp. In the nave the east window is 14th century with some pre-Reformation glass, including a Crucifixion and St Catherine and St Cecilia. Other items of interest are monuments commemorating two 14th century knights, two Sir William Disneys, father and son, and an alms box made from one piece of oak and dated 1639.

South of the church, on a great circular mound, stands a 19th century Hall. This is an ancient site which has yielded pre-Roman skeletons and artefacts believed to be of the New Stone Age. In the Hall grounds opposite the church is a stone which commemorates the building of a bridge at Bishopsbridge in 1451 by the Bishop of Lincoln. Some distance west of the church can be seen the ruins of almshouses built in 1675 for six poor people and, half a mile further on, a cross on a tree first erected in 1855 by T.A. Young after his stock had survived a cattle plague.

Moving eastwards we come to the neat and compact village of Kirkby with the church dedicated to St Andrew. The oldest work, tower and chancel, dates from the 13th century but the nave was rebuilt in 1790. In the chancel is a single and rare double piscina. Monuments commemorate John Wildbore (1398) and his mother. The chancel stands at a slight angle to the nave and the east window is also asymmetrical. Both these facts have traditional explanations and significance. In the churchyard is the base of an old cross. Kirkby 60 years ago could boast a blacksmith, cycle repairer, miller, joiner and undertaker. One business has flourished; the cycle shop has grown into a large and very efficient garage. Until recently a National school building of 1822 stood in the village but it has been swept away in a small housing development.

Osgodby (Osgotebi in the Domesday Book) is a long, straggling village to the south of Kingerby Beck. Buildings of note include the Methodist chapel (ex-Wesleyan) of 1897 in red brick and still in regular use for worship and Sunday school; the Primitive Methodist chapel building of the mid 19th century is now used as a garage and store. There is also a row of cottages of about 1840 built of locally handmade brick by a speculative builder, Nash, of Market Rasen. These cottages have been modernised but the front elevation is little changed from the original. The most interesting building is the Roman Catholic chapel built in 1793 to comply with anti-Catholic penal laws that were still on the Statute Book. It was the kind of chapel in which Roman Catholics had worshipped during the harsh days of legal repression. Osgodby chapel is one of the few late 18th century Roman Catholic chapels left in England.

The names of two lanes leading off the main road through the village are indicative of former industry but now there is no sheepwash in Washdyke Lane and no mill on Mill Lane. In Osgodby is a County primary school which takes pupils from this and neighbouring parishes. Further east, on Osgodby Moor, are extensive Forestry Commission woods. These occupy the site of more ancient forests which existed in the 17th century.

On the eastern boundary of the parish lies the hamlet of Usselby. Here, at the end of a narrow lane from the main road (A46), stands St Margaret's church. This small building contains some medieval masonry but was remodelled in the 18th and 19th centuries. Modern panelling behind the altar commemorates members of the Machin family. A nearby Georgian Hall was, in the 1830s, in the possession of the Right Hon C. Tennyson d'Eyncourt, the uncle of Alfred Lord Tennyson the poet laureate.

In the four villages of this parish friendship and community spirit are very much alive. There are various active societies. Newcomers are always welcome and invited to join. This is a mixed, warm-hearted, neighbourly group of villages for all age groups and hopefully will continue to be so for many years to come.

Kirton Holme 🐦

The village is small with a population of about 370. With some of the most fertile land in the East of England, farming was the main industry in this area with crops of cauliflowers, cabbage, potatoes, sugar beet and some cereals; with tied cottages and men and women working in the fields. Now some of the small farms have been swallowed up by larger ones and the fresh vegetable marketing is being replaced to a degree by pre-packed vegetables which are sent to supermarkets. Recently various factories and workshops have been built, including a potato and onion co-operative dealing with English and foreign produce, and a local firm of vegetable pre-packers. The local school, long since closed, is now a lorry trailer building firm; also in the village is a firm making small gears for vehicles – all firms providing some work. Farming is mainly done by the farmer and his sons with very little outside labour.

Very few houses will be built in the near future in Kirton Holme. The few council houses at Kirton Holme were built over 35 years ago.

The village has one public house/restaurant. In the centre of the village is the shop and post office, a valuable service which we hope we never lose.

The village church, named Christ Church, was once the Methodist chapel. From the outside it has altered little but inside it is like most Anglican churches. The church is part of a group of six parishes, namely Amber Hill, Holland Fen, Brothertoft, Langrick, Wildmore and Kirton Holme.

In 1988 the church hall was renovated by volunteers and won second prize in the Lincolnshire Village Ventures competition sponsored by Shell (UK).

A drain runs through the village where nowadays ducks seem to stay and 'multiply' and occasionally there are swans.

Kirton in Holland 🐦

The fact that Kirton in Holland has a Town Hall, a Town Football Club and a Town Brass Band, indicates immediately that it is a large village, though no longer the third largest settlement in Lincolnshire, as it was in the reign of Elizabeth I. Situated four miles south of Boston on the

A16, this former market town has a population of around 4,000 and is still noted for its long association with the twin industries of agriculture and horticulture.

A busy, bustling village to those using its wide main street fringed with a useful variety of shops, banks and other offices of modern life, it is nevertheless surrounded by areas of marshland which introduce a sense of desolation and timelessness.

Mentioned in the Domesday Book and long identified in various forms of the word 'Chircetune', Kirton's early development owed much to attempts at draining the area by successive invaders and then to the taming of its inhabitants by the Normans.

Plagues, floods and riots have taken their toll of Kirton through the years with disease wiping out 10% of the population in 1590 and floods necessitating the raising of the sea bank in 1820 and the building of a second defence further inland some years later. Until the mid 17th century livestock dominated local farming but the Enclosures Act saw changes which so incensed those who kept geese on the marshes that rioting took place, men were killed, animals poisoned and farm buildings fired. Once the initial anger was over, future generations of Kirton people benefited from the more habitable and profitable land which was produced.

The marshes are much enjoyed by wildfowlers and naturalists today but the villagers no longer flock there on Bank Holidays for sport and refreshment at the Old Boat and Gun. Lush samphire is, however, still collected for boiling or pickling.

The church of St Peter and St Paul which dominates the centre of Kirton has 13th century origins. Originally it was of cruciform design and extremely large. But in 1804 architect William Hayward used gunpowder to blow up much of the delapidated building. The transepts were destroyed, the chancel and nave were shortened and a new tower was built at the west end.

Interesting features inside include a memorial window to the memory of J.S. Paulson, a local lad killed in the First World War, and a scroll in appreciation of the work done by Dame Sarah Swift from Blossom Hall, Kirton Skeldyke, who was Matron in Chief of all Red Cross Hospitals in the same war and founder of the Royal College of Nursing. The beautiful kneelers in the church are the handiwork of local ladies, many commemorating friends and relatives.

Other buildings of note include the King's Head, a 17th century former ale house; Harvey House, an impressive Georgian home overlooking the war memorial; the Hunt almshouses in Willington Road; the Speak almshouses in London Road; and the Town Hall, built in 1911 to commemorate the Coronation of George V.

Formed in 1870 and one of the oldest in the country, Kirton Town Brass Band has played at all major events including fetes and festivals, sports days, coronations and jubilees. The band played while 1,600 sat down to tea on the village green to mark Queen Victoria's Jubilee in 1897 and in the 1960s its prowess was such that it reached the final stages of national competition in London.

A new primary school, opened in 1975, has released buildings for other community activities while the secondary school, renamed the Middlecott School, reminds one that Sir Thomas Middlecott established a grammar school in Kirton in 1624 which continued, albeit with something of a chequered career, until 1919. The Ministry of Agriculture's Advisory Service now occupies the site and has an Experimental Horticultural Station not far away where important work on bulbs and other crops is carried out.

Synonymous with agriculture as with the village as a whole, is the name of William Dennis, benefactor of the Town Hall and founder of a family business still flourishing today. Born in 1841, he built up a huge potato enterprise and supplied all the potatoes eaten at a dinner for the poor of London to mark King Edward VII's coronation. When William lay dying in 1924, the street outside his Kirton home was covered with straw to deaden any noise.

New houses have mushroomed on the outskirts of the village while food packing plants and agricultural machinery businesses mingle with the older homes. A new fire station supersedes former premises in an old chapel and an indoor bowling rink, a garden centre and sheltered housing for the elderly have become established features.

As if to unite the past and present, the bells of Kirton church ring out once more after recent refurbishment and dedication. There are many memories of the past in Kirton but the future too seems well assured.

Langrick 🐝

Langrick is not so much a village as a parish. Bounded on the west and south by the river Witham and on the north and east by Castledyke drain, it has a thriving, yet dispersed population. Its two small, quite separate, groups of houses include a sub-post office and an inn – the

Ferry Boat, while midway between stands Langrick St Margaret with its church hall. There is no shop, school, doctor's surgery or vet. The Anglican parson, who looks after six parishes, lives in Brothertoft. In short, nothing about Langrick resembles the traditional English village.

Like so many of our fen parishes, Langrick is new. When the fen was finally drained and the land enclosed in 1802, Langrick had '....neither house nor inhabitant'. The brick church was built in 1818 and the ferry disappeared with the construction of the steel bridge over the river Witham in 1909. The river itself was finally straightened in 1833 though farmers still find reeds growing in its old meandering bed. From Tattershall the Great Northern Railway ran along the newly constructed river bank and left the Witham at Langrick station to loop across the countryside, rejoining the river and running on to the sluice bridge in Boston. Before Dr Beeching finally closed the line in the 1960s, Langrick boasted a signal box, level crossing, station, sidings and cattle loading dock. Now, only the station cottages remain.

Since the 1930s, 25 farming units have shrunk to ten, of which only about four are self-contained. There are, in addition, a few smallholdings of between 60 and 80 acres developed from those originally established by the County Council in 1912 but, even when these are taken into account, few of the dwellings in the parish now have occupants directly connected with farming.

A unique characteristic of the fen parishes in general and of Langrick in particular is their social structure which, because it is new, is marked by an absence of hereditary squires, parsons, doctors and school teachers, who in the past tended to guide the fortunes of the Domesday parishes. In Langrick everyone is a newcomer. The 'new' community has developed in its own way but is now as consolidated as that of many an older English village.

The Langrick community appears, in a physical sense, once every year at the harvest festival supper in the village hall. A more communal event it would be difficult to imagine. There is an excellent meal prepared by various ladies of the parish; someone with a sense of humour auctions the mounds of fruit, cakes and vegetables given for the occasion by the 60 or 70 people present and, as the evening wears on, the more recent residents meet the older hands while those who have moved to nearby parishes return to renew past friendships.

To the world at large, Langrick was probably best known to anglers who, after the Second World War, were drawn from as far afield as Sheffield and the mining towns of the Midlands by the good fishing the

89

river offered. The Ferry Boat Inn and the approaches to the Witham bridge were then often choked with traffic, especially when Langrick hosted the National Angling Championships. These days there are fewer anglers but in the season there are often a couple of big buses and a few cars at the bridge and the river banks once again become dotted with umbrellas.

Laughton 🦌

Laughton lies about three quarters of a mile to the west of the A159 road which links Gainsborough and Scunthorpe in the fertile Vale of Trent. Close by is Laughton Forest, a vast area of woodland which is mainly coniferous but with attractive belts of deciduous trees along the road margins. Much of the forest was originally open heathland and the Warren, adjoining Scotton Common, was a huge tract of blown sand with Hardwick Hill, rising to 132 ft, the highest point for miles around. Roman artefacts, including bronze, pottery and glass, were discovered earlier this century to the south of the hill and there is evidence that metal working was carried on here during the Roman occupation.

Laughton Wood, which is close to the A159, was planted between 1783 and 1789, while the majority of the commercial woodland, in the care of the Forestry Commission, was planted in the 1920s. Access to the forest is limited but an area to the north is now officially open to the public and there are many pleasant walks.

The village itself consists of old red brick farms and cottages interspersed with modern houses and bungalows clustered around the church. Although of medieval origin, All Saints' church was extensively and elaborately restored in 1896 by the eminent Victorian architect G.F. Bodley, and is well worth visiting. The original nave has a Norman north arcade while the south arcade is later, with good 14th century arches supported by octagonal pillars. The tower, erected in the 15th century, is topped by eight lofty pinnacles. The restoration work was made possible by the generosity of the Hon Mrs Meynell-Ingram in memory of her late husband, Hugo, who met an untimely death in the hunting field. The Meynell-Ingram family's connection with Laughton can be traced back to the time of Elizabeth I. Between the nave and the north aisle is a fine white marble effigy of the unfortunate Hugo Meynell-Ingram and this is a copy of the one on his canopied tomb in the church at Hoar Cross, the family seat in Staffordshire.

A much earlier monument on the south side of the nave is a table tomb with a splendid brass of an unknown knight in armour with a triple canopy above his head and a lion at his feet. There are inscriptions on the tomb to William Dalison, who was Sheriff of Lincolnshire in 1546, and also to his son. This tomb is a treat indeed for brass rubbers but requires extra-wide paper and great patience! The most recent addition to the church furnishings is the set of colourful kneelers worked by Women's Institute members and other parishioners.

Across the road from the church is an interesting grouping of school, school house and reading room. The latter now serves as a village meeting place. The school house is no longer occupied by school staff but the school itself flourishes and has long outgrown the original building dated 1841. Laughton Endowed School is notable as it was founded as a grammar school in 1566 by Roger Dalison, Precentor of Lincoln Cathedral, and has continued in constant use since that time.

The Primitive Methodist chapel in Scotter Road is a traditional red brick building dated 1927. It is the second chapel to occupy this site and the remains of an earlier one built in 1825 can be seen quite clearly in the car parking area close to the road. The present chapel, which stands up off the road surrounded by a lawned garden, has recently been refurbished inside. There were once two chapels in Laughton but the old Wesleyan chapel which stood in Morton Road closed some 70 years ago and was later demolished. It is interesting to note that a village the size of Laughton once supported three places of worship.

Laughton Hall, a fine five-bay, red brick Queen Anne house, stands well back from the road on the eastern fringe of the village and in doing so enjoys a certain air of aloofness.

The large house on the corner of Morton Road and Scotter Road is the Shooting Lodge and is owned by the Meynell estate. As its name implies it is the headquarters of the local shoot and is the scene of much activity on winter weekends as shooting parties assemble there.

On Blyton Road there is a remarkably well-stocked shop and post office and a pub. Originally a carpenter's shop, the Ingram Arms was opened in 1975, although there was a public house in the vicinity in the 19th century. This was closed over a hundred years ago on the orders of the lady of the manor who felt it encouraged licentiousness amongst the villagers!

Leadenham ✤

Leadenham village lies on the Lincolnshire Cliff, almost midway between Lincoln and Grantham. It was mentioned in the Domesday survey of 1086, when it already had its own church. The building of the present church began in about 1320.

In the 14th century a manor and a small plot of land were given to the prioress and nuns of the Abbey of Heveninges. (This manor was on the site of the present Leadenham stores.) In 1377 a small group of nuns was sent to Leadenham to live in the manor and to establish a hospice. Pilgrims on their way to visit the shrine of St Hugh at Lincoln would have been thankful to find a safe resting place for the night and to share meals prepared by the nuns from produce grown on their plot of land. This enclosure adjoining the present village hall is still known as Nun's Close.

At this time the wool trade was growing rapidly and wealthy merchants would travel through Leadenham with fleeces to sell in Lincoln. They too would stop at the hospice. They could afford to be generous and the church of St Swithun in Leadenham owes much to their generosity and patronage.

From these early beginnings Leadenham has grown into the busy village of today. The school started as a dame school and in 1857 a proper school opened on land given by General Reeve. This was supported by voluntary contributions.

The original houses in the village were built of local stone and centred round the crossroads. Over the years, growth has taken place, mainly along the line of the A607 road between Lincoln and Grantham. Other building materials have been used at the north end of the village but the main impression still remains of stone-built houses surrounded by farmland.

Eleven farmers are involved in agriculture in the Leadenham area. They are mainly tenant farmers who lease the land from the Reeves' Leadenham estate. The land on the heath towards Sleaford is limestone based, drains well and is easily worked, while the fields towards Newark are heavy clay based and require a good deal of drainage and ditching. A large part of the farming is arable with wheat and barley as the main grain crops. Grass is grown for silage and hay for winter feed. Oil seed rape and sugar beet are also grown in quantity. Only a small proportion of the land is used for grazing sheep and cattle, the latter being mainly Charolais and other Continental crosses.

A railway line used to run through Leadenham, until it was closed in the 1960s. As there was a long siding at Leadenham station, Queen Victoria's train used to stop here overnight on her way to Scotland. In the Second World War the Royal Train stopped here when members of the Royal Family were visiting nearby RAF stations such as Scampton and Waddington.

The Reeve family have lived at Leadenham House since 1738 and still own much of the surrounding land. Leadenham is one of the few remaining estate villages in the county. The squire has always been patron of the church and has not only appointed the rector, but has, down the ages, encouraged the villagers to care for and support the church.

Leadenham has a village shop and post office, which stocks a wide variety of goods besides the normal groceries. Various vans also serve the village. The fishmonger calls weekly as does a greengrocer. The butcher calls twice a week and the baker three times. Besides this the mobile bank calls every week and the mobile library calls fortnightly.

Many meetings have been held in the village hall by the Ministry of Transport and others in attempts to solve the traffic problem in the village. Schemes for a bypass have been under discussion since the 1930s and it seems at times as if the problem will never be resolved. The steadily increasing volume and weight of traffic thundering through the village centre causes damage to property and is a hazard to anyone trying to cross the main roads.

For recreation in the village there is a well maintained playing field with tennis, cricket and bowls. There is a lively Over 60s club and also regular bingo sessions. Two hostelries serve the village – the George Hotel, with accommodation and restaurant, and the Leadenham Arms.

Leasingham 🐝

Leasingham is an expanding village 15 miles south of Lincoln, two miles from Cranwell and two miles from its nearest market town of Sleaford. A milestone near the church says it is 117 miles from London.

A village with a wide range of architecture, there are houses dating back to the 1700s, some very well preserved with original windows, doors and latches. Like all villages it has, over the years, acquired more and more estates to house the ever-expanding population. One of the oldest houses is the Manor built in the 18th century, which boasts its own ghost.

The church of St Andrew is over 700 years old, although it is certain that a church existed on the same site before this. One of the most striking features is the tower and an Angel porch. Three of the four bells date back to 1617. Like most old churches it is constantly in need of funds for maintenance.

The local chapel, naturally, is situated half way down Chapel Lane. It is a reasonably new building, light and modern, and is attached to the Wesleyan Reform Union.

Dating back to the 1600s is the local public house, the Duke of Wellington. It is constantly being renovated and extended but still manages to retain its old world charm.

A stone's throw from the church is the village school, once a two-roomed stone building, now a five-classroomed modern bright school for the numerous red and grey clad children. It even has its own playing field.

Shopping facilities include a butcher's shop, post office, general stores, farm shop, hairdresser's and a small charity shop run for the NSPCC. The local playing field provides exercise space for the energetic, with a football pitch, bowling greens and a children's corner.

Although the name Leasingham means a village situated amidst pastures and meadows it is not now a very rural village, having few privately owned farms. Houses seem to have taken the place of stackyards and cattle sheds, although the outer boundaries are still surrounded by farmland. In one area of the village residents regularly see pheasants, owls and plenty of the usual bird life, but the baaing of sheep and the lowing of cattle is no longer heard.

On the Sleaford side of the village is the rookery, where rooks have built their nests for years. The legend says the nearer the birds build to the top of the tree the better the summer. Several chestnut trees with their white candles in the spring have, in the autumn, supplied generations of children with conkers.

Legbourne

The village of Legbourne is situated on the edge of the Lincolnshire Wolds some three and a half miles south-east of the market town of Louth, on the A157 road, and is within easy reach of the East Coast resort of Mablethorpe and the various open beaches along that stretch of coast.

It is not known how long there has been a settlement at Legbourne, although there would have been farms and houses here when the Cistercian priory was built before the reign of King John and when All Saints' church was built in 1380.

The priory was founded by Robert Fitz Gilbert de Lekeburn in the 12th century. It was occupied by nuns and when it was finally dissolved in the reign of Henry VIII, it is recorded that it had a yearly income of £38 8s 4d, in those days a considerable amount of money. The site of the priory is in the grounds of Legbourne Abbey, at present a private house, the only visible remains of the original building being some earth mounds.

Situated in the centre of the village, All Saints' church has two unusual features. Firstly, it is constructed entirely of one period type and secondly, it has a chantry nave, a small chapel where a priest who had been commissioned to say private prayers on the death of a wealthy person, could carry out these duties. The church clock was presented to the village by Thomas Cheney Garfitt in 1890 and, in 1897, the original peal of three bells was increased to five by him to commemorate the Diamond Jubilee of Queen Victoria.

The village pump, an imposing canopied and pinnacled stone structure standing in front of the church, was built by Canon J. Overton in 1877 in memory of his mother. The pump was the principal supply of water to the village until 1953, when mains water finally came to the village.

Legbourne Church Aided primary school, which also stands in the centre of the village, dates from 1863. Built for 45 boys and 65 girls at a cost of £300, it is still a centre of primary education, with children coming in from neighbouring villages and even from Louth.

Before the infamous Beeching cuts closed so many of the railway systems, the East Lincolnshire section of the Great Northern Railway, built in 1863, ran to the west of the village. Legbourne station was situated on the A157 road, just outside the village on the Louth side and, although the level crossing is no longer in existence, the old station house, now a private residence, can be seen on the right just before entering the village. The platform and a new building, constructed in the form of an engine shed, houses a most interesting railway museum which is well worth a visit. This, together with the adjacent picnic area, provides a most convenient stop for visitors.

In recent years small pockets of new housing development have somewhat altered the original character of the village, which has always been principally a farming community. One new road, Alfred Smith Way, has been so named in memory of a Legbourne man, Alfred Smith, who gave his life to pioneer work carried out on the use of X rays. He eventually suffered from the effects of radiation and from 1913 onwards his life was one of intense suffering, having had one leg amputated and being half blind. Having exhausted his savings he was compelled to sell his home and was granted a small pension by the Carnegie Hero Fund which enabled him to come to Legbourne to live in an old army hut, where he took up poultry farming to support his family. Alfred Smith died in 1933 and was buried in Grimsby.

Legbourne Mill was built by Thomas Davy in 1847, after the original post mill had been destroyed by fire. It and the surrounding buildings have now been converted into private residences.

The village is well served by the post office and general store, situated in Post Office Row adjacent to the church and, at the far end of the village, the Queen's Head pub which still retains its old village 'local' atmosphere.

Little Cawthorpe

Little Cawthorpe is situated three miles south-east of Louth, just off the A157 Louth to Mablethorpe road. It is a small community tucked away on the edge of the Wolds, and the population is almost the same as it was 150 years ago. It is almost entirely residential, one farm only remaining of the five of 50 years ago.

There is a nice mix of age groups, families and retired people. People travel to work in Louth and further afield to Lincoln and the Humber Bank. There are some attractive well-kept older residences, as well as modern bungalows and houses. The village is situated round a square with a large green area in the centre.

The local inn (the Royal Oak) and the church are meeting places for the villagers, although the inn attracts many outsiders especially at weekends and holiday times. This is not surprising as the village is very pretty with its high hedges, narrow lanes and well kept gardens. The village is well-wooded, although the magnificent elms on the green surrounding the Royal Oak became victims of Dutch elm disease.

A very attractive area of the village is the one which includes the manor house, old vicarage and St Helen's church. This area is always well kept by the local residents. Here also is the source of the Long Eau; before the area was transformed into an attractive pond, it was possible to count at least seven springs running out of the bank. The pond is kept in good order by local residents who are justly proud of this feature which attracts mallards and moorhens as well as a few fish. To some local residents this is still 'The Springs'.

The manor house is a mellow red brick house built in 1673. It has diamond-shaped chimney stacks and mullioned windows with four Dutch gables. A Victorian letter box is set in one of the gateposts. The old vicarage, built in 1855, is a well kept, almost unchanged building but has not been used as such for many years.

St Helen's church, set on the hill, is also a red brick building, rebuilt about 130 years ago. Here if you turn left you take the road to the next small village of Muckton. A small settlement at the bottom of a steep hill is called Muckton Bottom but is still in Cawthorpe parish. The views across the middle-march to the sea are quite spectacular from this road.

If you turn right at Cawthorpe church the road, Pinfold Lane, takes you past a number of modern houses and bungalows until you see a pair of semi-detached houses built on the site of the old pinfold or animal compound where stray cattle were held.

The Long Eau, mentioned earlier, flows through Little Cawthorpe valley by the gardens of private houses until it appears again under the bridge by the ford. This is also approached by the high hedges of Buston Lane and leads to the part of the village described earlier. Here you also find the entrance to the inn and admire the view to the top of the hill, a popular subject for photographers. The Beck-side, the footpath by the side of the stream, is a very pleasant walk and a short cut to the nearby village of Legbourne. Here it is possible to enjoy a walk down Wood Lane and to return to the Muckton road by a sign-posted footpath with open views of the surrounding countryside.

The residents of Little Cawthorpe were delighted to win the CPRE award in 1988 for the Lincolnshire Best Kept Small Village Competition. An oak tree planted on the grassy area near the Royal Oak was the prize donated to the village.

Long Bennington 🐿

Long Bennington lies between Newark and Grantham on the Lincolnshire/Nottinghamshire border. Settlement in the area dates from the Bronze Age. Archaeological excavations in 1972-1975 revealed a Bronze Age burial ground and the sites of Roman villas.

The Cistercian Order built a priory here in 1150, and there were monks at Bennington until 1642. Nothing remains of the actual structure of the priory, but the sites of the fish ponds (which provided a source of food for the monks) can still be seen.

The church was built before 1086, for the Domesday Book recorded 'a church with a priest'. Today St Swithun's is an amalgam of styles from the 12th to 19th centuries, with the little that remains of the earlier church incorporated in its south doorway.

In the latter half of the 19th century a plan, approved by the Bishop, to rebuild the church in the centre of the village was put to all the householders. The response was favourable, but alas the £5,000 needed to carry out the work could not be raised. And so the church still stands where it always did; in a pleasant, open position, being almost the last house at the Grantham end of the village. In its churchyard are the graves of four Canadian airmen who died whilst serving at a nearby RAF station during the Second World War. The bodies of Polish airmen, also buried there, were transferred to the Polish cemetery when it was opened in Newark. A reminder of the futility of war, their graves are regularly tended by one of the villagers.

But there was to be a church in the centre of the village after all, for after a disagreement with the vicar in 1890 the lady of the manor had one built, at a cost of £650. She also at her own expense provided a curate who took the services. These were held on Sunday and Friday evenings, and the bell was tolled at 10 each morning for prayers. The church had a small hall, for use as a reading room, and was called St James'. When it was no longer needed as a church, it was transferred to the village by deed of gift for use as a village hall, retaining limited ecclesiastical use. The name was changed to St James' Hall and Reading Room (but always referred to as 'The Village Hall and the Iron Room').

Some first time visitors must have wondered if they had got to the church by mistake, as with its lancet windows and steep roof it was not the conventional picture of a village hall. But it will unfortunately not be seen in the future. For in the early hours of the 8th May in 1987, the floor, roof and stage area of the main hall were damaged by fire; and though it was confined to one section it was not thought feasible to merely repair and patch up, demolition and rebuilding being the only answer.

Long Bennington must always have been a lively village, standing as it did on the old medieval route from London to York. Never more so than in the Civil War, when it had Royalist Newark on one hand and Parliamentarian Grantham on the other. Its inhabitants would be used to the sight of horses and carriages passing through, or stopping at one of the coaching inns, the White Lion maybe, which catered for all tastes, being an inn at the front and a dairy and bakery at the rear. Main Street, which runs the length of the village, is the ideal setting for the Georgian and other old houses (the oldest dating from 1550), which stand on it.

An increase in the number of houses has meant an increase in the number of families with children needing school places and the school, built in 1843, could not accommodate them all. So, unlike many Lincolnshire villages, whose schools have been closed, Long Bennington is now the possessor of a well equipped, modern school. Those other 'endangered species' of village life, the shop and the post office, are also so far still surviving.

There are five working farms within the village and a mill, which unfortunately, owing to the river having been diverted some years ago, no longer uses water power.

Three thriving family businesses have developed here too. A couturier, who makes glamorous clothes for showbusiness personalities, a maker of carriages for the growing sport of carriage driving popularised by the participation of a member of the Royal Family, and a firm which specialises in the making and repair of a particular type of agricultural equipment. All of them, though small, regularly export to Europe and America.

Long Sutton

No, not long because of the length along the main road, but because of the length of the original parish from north to south. Long Sutton was mentioned in the Domesday Book and certainly existed prior to that as the Roman Bank (old sea bank) protected it from the sea on north and east sides, and it stands between marsh and fen. Bull Hill is 20½ ft above sea level and Pop Bottle Bridge 10 ft (yes, there is a pop bottle top built into the bridge).

There was an old wooden church prior to the existing one. St Mary's is 800 years old with the chancel, aisles and magnificent spire of lead in a herringbone pattern on wood. This is an attraction for visitors, particularly during the flower festival which has a different theme each year.

In recent years the Butterfly Park has proved very popular indeed with additional facilities and attractions each year.

Visitors should note several Georgian houses, some with lovely fanlights. There is a good selection of shops centred around High Street, Market Street and the Market Place where an old established market is held each Friday. Excellent sporting facilities are available. There is an adult school and evening classes are held at the Peele school. A new primary school was built in 1984 – both schools having good playing fields.

There has been much building with attractively planned new estates, with more planned, but there are good open spaces and sports grounds in and around the centre.

The names of some of the new roads refer to events and people of the past. Lancaster Drive is near to what was known as John of Gaunt's House. John of Gaunt was lord of the manor of Sutton, Holland and owned much of the rich land around. There are also Turpin Way, Saddlers Way and York Ride. Although it is now disputed that Dick Turpin rode from London to York, it is thought that he certainly visited Long Sutton, staying at an ale house which was situated in the yard behind the present post office.

Ludborough & North Ormsby

Ludborough, population 184, is two miles north of Utterby on the A16 road. It is primarily a farming community, but has many residents who commute to Grimsby.

The church of St Mary was substantially rebuilt in 1858 after the earlier building was severely damaged in a gale.

Ludborough was the important centre of the Wapentake of Ludborough in Danish times. This included, among others, the villages of Utterby and North Ormsby, and was the smallest wapentake in Lincolnshire.

It is the site of a large medieval deserted village, and although there has been some building on the site, outlines of old buildings can still be seen. The desertion of the village was not due to the Black Death or other catastrophe, but to changes in farming, when the herds and flocks were moved down to the drained marshes, and also because of the enclosures.

The name of the main landowner and lord of the manor was Livesey, whose name is seen on the local public house, The Livesey Arms. One of the farms grows excellent soft fruit where you can 'Pick Your Own' in the summer.

North Ormsby, or Nun Ormsby as it was once known, is situated south of Ludborough. The population in 1981 was just 47. This hamlet consists of a manor house and the houses and cottages of the farm workers. There is also a pheasantry which was started in 1968, for the rearing of game birds.

The ancient church of St Helen was substantially rebuilt in 1848, but sadly is now closed and converted back into a dwelling.

North Ormsby used to be a much larger village and was the site of a Gilbertine abbey, which was founded in the reign of King Stephen by Sir Oswald-de-Ormsby. After the Dissolution of the Monasteries, it was granted by Henry VIII to Sir Robert Heneage. All traces of the abbey have now gone, though the outline of the deserted village which served the abbey can be seen very clearly from the nearby road. An archaeological dig took place some years ago, but the results have not been published. There is a statue, known as The White Lady of Ormsby, which stands on the site and is said to be of Roman origin. There are also six Saxon graves in the village.

Maltby-le-Marsh 🌾

The village of Maltby-le-Marsh is situated on the A1104, two miles west of Mablethorpe and five miles north of Alford.

The church of All Saints still stands, a church having been mentioned in the Domesday Book, though it has been rebuilt at least three times. It comprises a nave, south porch, chancel and tower. The tower is about 250 years old, and the chancel 200 years old, but the nave is very much older.

In the chancel is the recumbent effigy of a man in armour, thought to be one of the early knights killed in a duel at Earl's Bridge, which is the eastern boundary of Maltby-le-Marsh.

The rectory was built in 1839, and the first incumbent was the Rev Robert Allott BA, who lived there for 55 years. In 1847 he built a Church school, with a house adjoining for the schoolmistress. It was closed in 1922 when it had 72 pupils. The rectory was sold away from the church in 1938 and at present is a private nursing home.

There were three schools at one time in Maltby, long before Mablethorpe had even one. In 1705 Mrs Anne Bolle 'gave and devised a farm' to pay for a schoolmaster to teach poor children their catechism. The school house was still in good repair in 1837, but has since been demolished. It stood near the present farmhouse of School Farm. The Anne Bolle charity is still used to provide money for educational purposes for village children, and '40 shillings' is still distributed to the elderly at Christmas.

The Methodist church stands near the village centre, and was built in 1873 to replace the Wesleyan chapel which was immediately opposite. This is now a private dwelling, 'The Chantry'. A school room at the rear is used by many organisations, as it is the only room in the village available for public use.

There is a manor house over 250 years old, and although it is no longer manorial, it is an impressive building situated on the western boundary. Part of the moat is still visible. It is said that there was an underground passage connecting the manor to the Baptist chapel, which was built in 1736 by the occupant of the manor. It was sold in the late 1800s, though it was still used as a place of worship. In the early 1970s it was once again sold, and is now a private residence.

There are two public houses. The Crown was once three small cottages and until the late 1940s the western boundary of the car park was the site of the village smithy. The Turk's Head, another old building of interest, was built in the 18th century. It is reputed to be haunted by the ghost of a First World War soldier.

In the heart of the village is the shop, built in 1780. There have been many additions over the years, and in 1909 it was granted a post office licence, still current. Opposite is a recently established private printing works.

The windmill, built in the 1840s, was working until the 1950s. It also included a bakery. These buildings are now the Old Mill Restaurant, which also offers accommodation.

On the eastern boundary of the village used to stand the water pumping station. This was demolished in 1968 and a one million gallon reservoir built in its place to serve Mablethorpe and the surrounding area. The old house on the site is now privately owned.

Nearby is Willow Farm Caravan Park, which has grown from two caravans in the 1950s to having over 100 on site in 1989.

There are preservation orders on four properties in the village, the manor, Dovecote House, the dovecote, and the Baptist chapel.

Marshchapel 🌿

Marshchapel was once part of the parish of Fulstow. As the sea receded and more people found a living at the east end of the parish, a chapel was built. The first written evidence of this was in 1387, when the rector of Fulstow was directed to find a vicar for 'The Chapel in the Marsh'.

The western boundary separating the two parishes was drawn on an old watercourse, which is now roughly the route of the old Louth Navigation Canal. The southern boundary follows a pre-Roman track known as The Salters Way.

Salt was the chief industry from pre-Roman times until the 16th century, evidence of which abounds on the eastern side of the ancient sea bank, shown as undulations in the fields. North Lane goes up and down like a huge switch-back. The sea bank is now the main road, known as Sea Dyke Way, and the northern boundary follows one of the many watercourses of the marsh drainage system. The retreating foreshore of the Humber estuary marks the eastern boundary.

The land is light silt in the east, running to heavy clay in the west, mostly now under the plough. There is still evidence of medieval strip farming in the grass fields near the church; it was enclosed in 1841.

The Perpendicular church, early 15th century, dedicated to St Mary, is a very handsome one, and has been called 'The Cathedral of the Marsh'. It has three bells. The treble bell, recast in 1919, bears the names of the eight men of the parish who died in the First World War. The largest bell, called 'John', is dated 1584 and the other, 1689. The church was built all in one piece and has some fine carved bench ends and a rood screen, possibly a relic from Louth Abbey.

The Old Hall at Marshchapel was built in 1720, during the reign of George I, on land which belonged to Sir Joseph Banks, explorer and naturalist, who accompanied Captain Cook to Australia. The original house was gable-ended, but wings were added in 1780 and 1820. High ceilings were fashionable c1820, which explains the irregular windows in the west wing.

The first owners were the Loft family. William Loft was an MP for Grimsby, and Loft Street was renamed Victoria Street at the Golden Jubilee. Another William Loft sunk one of the first artesian wells in the district in 1794, lined with beautiful hand-fashioned copper tubing; it still exists. Mary Loft, who died in the late 1700s, had 19 children, all of whom died during infancy – the sad row of little graves can be seen in Marshchapel churchyard.

The Victorian Methodist chapel standing on the main street was recently restored with grant aid and now also serves as a community centre. Inside is a plaque commemorating an earlier chapel of 1795.

The village hall was built in 1958. This replaced an old Army Nissen hut from the war years, when the whole village was used as an army camp prior to the Normandy landings. The two largest houses of the village were commandeered, Campo as an RAF hospital and Clyde House as Army Officers' quarters.

A windmill stands on the east of the main road. It was originally a post mill, erected by Charles Ryland before 1595 on a site gifted to him by the Monarch. The mill served the neighbouring villages and remained working until 1837, when it was replaced by the present mill, erected by George Bull Bros of Hull, to the order of the Addiscombe family of Grimsby. The present mill was a round tower of three floors, built of red brick; it had four sailed patents, single shuttered and turned by hand with chains. There were three pairs of stones and the mill ground some 120 quarters of corn per week. It ceased working after being damaged by a great storm on 6th January 1922 – the machinery was removed and sold for scrap by the then owner, Mr Wray. The present owner, Capt V. Sheffield, replaced the doors and windows and made the tower waterproof.

The school was first built halfway between Marshchapel and Northcotes in 1838, serving both parishes. In 1870, when Northcotes got its own school, the building was removed, the bricks, tiles and windows were carted to Marshchapel and rebuilt on its present site, following to a great extent the original design. Over the years the building has been re-roofed, re-windowed and modernised, but in general still keeps its original character.

104

St Mary's Church, Marshchapel

As villages go, there are very good services – three grocer's (one of which is the post office), a butcher's, fish shop and garage. Two other important places are the Greyhound and the White Horse Inn. Domino, darts and pool teams are run from both, and they both serve meals. A great deal of charity work centres on and around the pubs.

Martin Dales 🐝

The area of Martin Dales can be defined by the river Witham on its eastern boundary, Blankney Dales to the north, Walcott Dales to the south, and merging into Martin Fen and Timberland Fen to the west.

If there has to be a centre to Martin Dales one would say Kirkstead, as it is commonly known by locals and the many hundreds of fishermen and women who visit this river bank area, between June and March every year. This also happens to be the most heavily populated area with an estate of council bungalows and a large number of caravans, with all the usual amenities. There is also a large car park and the head-quarters of the Angling Clubs Association.

In Church Road one will find St Hugh's church hall. This hall started life as a garage, which was bought and turned into a church hall to replace the old church when it was pulled down, because of its age and poor state of repair. The money to buy the hall had been raised by the people of the Dales, by sheer hard work and determination to have their own place of worship once again. The church hall is part of the Trinity church, Martin.

There is still a family-run garage in the area called Kirkstead Bridge garage, taking its name from the bridge which spans the river Witham. This bridge was built to replace the old railway bridge, which in its day had to be swung open to allow river traffic to pass through, causing traffic holdups on either side. The railway station has been closed for many years.

There is a public house, a fishing tackle shop and a builder's yard near to the bridge on the Martin Dales side. When the grocery store closed, the Martin Dales post office was transferred to the small grocer's shop in Mill Lane, which is over the river near to Woodhall Spa.

Martin Dales is a very rural area. The main occupation is naturally agriculture and is mainly arable, growing cereals, sugar beet, potatoes, beans for stock feed, and a relatively new crop giving a beautiful yellow carpet of flowers from May to July, oil seed rape. There are a number of small farms owned by the Lincolnshire County Council and rented by tenants, and larger privately owned farms. But it is inevitable that with modern farming methods and new machinery the numbers employed on the land have decreased and other employment has been sought by redundant farm workers.

The Waterside Methodist chapel is on the roadway which runs along-side the river and is still in use today with a very active Sunday school.

Marton 🐚

Marton has seen much history in the making for it lies where the Roman legions would have crossed the Trent. The ford they used, dating back to Hadrian's time, can still be seen in periods of severe drought.

The river used to be quite busy with tugs towing strings of barges to Lincoln or Boston, but anything other than a pleasure boat is a rare sight nowadays. The Egre, or tidal bore, reaches as far as Marton and beyond and to see a high one is quite an experience. There is no official public footpath along the river bank but one is signposted via the cliff top. Following this path gives a lovely view of the river meandering through the marshes with the occasional fisherman enjoying the peace.

Prominent also are the power stations, standing on the Nottingham side of the river, which are responsible for this area being dubbed 'Megawatt Valley'. Almost at the end of the clifftop path stands the now derelict windmill, built in 1799 but largely dismantled in 1926. A corn warehouse, a malthouse and a wharf to serve them also stood here when it was a port, hence the name Trentport – but nothing remains of these today. The cluster of dwellings was demolished in more recent years and a group of caravans occupy the site now.

The A156 road is the High Street and here for 116 years stood the attractive village school with its chequered brickwork and delightful little bell tower. The school was demolished and St Margaret's home for the elderly was built on the site. A new school was built on Tillbridge Lane in 1962.

Almost in the centre of the village stands the church of St Margaret of Antioch. Much of the work of both Normans and Saxons is retained. Its tall unbuttressed tapering tower was built in the 11th century. It has walls entirely of fine herringbone work right up to the bellchamber. The chancel walls also contain much herringbone work and its arch and heavy mouldings was made by the Normans. The north arcade of two wide bays comes from the close of the Norman period and the rest of the church belongs to the 13th century. The tall cross in the churchyard, restored and used as a war memorial, is thought to have been an old market butter cross.

Marton Wesleyan chapel dates back to 1814 and still flourishes today. A smaller Primitive Methodist chapel in Wapping Lane has now been demolished.

A Lincolnshire directory published in 1876 names the keepers of three public houses in Marton, but of these only one remains today, the Ingleby Arms with its pleasant gardens and play area. The White Swan has been demolished and the Railway Inn in Tillbridge Lane has been a private house for almost half a century.

The large house at the bottom of the hill where Tillbridge Lane runs down into the village was known as the Black Swan and was a coaching inn until 1860. Travellers called here to change horses and take refreshment before continuing their journey. Dick Turpin is reputed to have spent the night here on his way to York. The stables and interior arrangements of the house remain much the same though necessary modernisation has been carried out. The old mounting block stood outside until a few years ago when it was removed for safety reasons.

During the removal of a fireplace various papers and visiting cards were discovered. These had dropped down behind the old mantelpiece and one of them had been there for 133 years. There was also some most interesting writing scratched on a windowpane and dated 1779. Unfortunately a traffic accident caused the window to be broken and though there are photographs the original is lost.

Marton still has a village post office and a local shop, a fish shop and restaurant, a newsagent, a milk retailer and a garage but unfortunately no longer a petrol station. All employment has to be sought elsewhere, mainly in Gainsborough, Lincoln or at one of the power stations.

Many new dwellings have been built in recent years, but because there are few large families nowadays the population remains at between 400 and 500.

Minting ￼

The village was mentioned in the Domesday Book as 'the Mintings'. Actually what is now called Top Minting (on the opposite side of Mill Lane from the Midge, Mill Lane being the border between Hatton and Minting at that point) is quite a long way from Minting village. Minting covered an acreage of 2,543 but is now less as Minting Park is now in the parish of Gautby.

There was a Benedictine priory in the village but where it was exactly is not known for sure. The site often shown for it on present maps was actually one of the sites of the medieval village. There were great outcries against the morals of those in the priory, said to be living a life of debauchery, gambling and consorting with loose women. Bishop Grostete was certainly very outspoken in trying to get these wicked practices stopped. Eventually the priory was annexed and handed over to one of the Yorkshire priories to administer, until the Reformation when it was disbanded.

The present St Andrew's church was rebuilt by Mr Evan Christian, an architect, in 1863. Lord Monson of Burton owned lands in Minting and in 1779 an agreement was made to exchange these with the Church for lands which they owned at Burton.

It is reputed that the local pub – The Sebastapol – got its name when an inquest was held there on a soldier found dead in the area. As the pub had no name and the battle had recently taken place it was given its present name.

In 1881 the population of Minting was 347, but a hundred years later was only 169. Today the population is around 220. Local services have dwindled. There is no longer a village school or shop and the post office opens only three half days a week.

Morton (nr Bourne)

Morton is a large village of brick and stone on the very edge of the fens. The long village street lined with attractive houses leads up to the west front of the church, dedicated to St John the Baptist. The church dominates the east of the village and resembles a miniature cathedral. The little priest's door in the south wall of the chancel may be late 12th century and belonged to an earlier church. Features of the church are the original panelled and carved west door, the beautiful stained glass windows and the huge clock face. With a clear view it is possible to tell the time a distance of a mile away.

Crossing the A15 the newer part of the village to the west is overlooked by richly wooded uplands.

Down the long main street is a butcher's shop, the old school, the village hall, the Baptist chapel and the post office. The old school has recently been converted into a very desirable residence. The village hall was once a Methodist chapel. The Grange, with its beautiful gardens and buildings is the home of Mr John Richardson, farmer and his family. Many charitable events take place in these grounds. A beautiful thatched cottage has recently and expertly been re-thatched. There is also a church hall and two general stores.

In the 1880s there were at least 17 farmers in Morton and Hanthorpe. Many of them had other trades. Daniel Baker doubled as a blacksmith, William Hall was both farmer and coal merchant and William Clark was a farmer, butcher and landlord of the Five Bells. Samuel Eayes was grocer, baker and draper; Richard Steel, chemist and druggist and grocer; Williamson Bros were grocers, bakers and corn millers. The record for multiple jobs was held by Jesse Stow, who was schoolmaster, rate collector, vestry clerk, land measurer, organist and insurance agent!

The Sunday after 6th July is known as Feast Sunday. Until recent years it was the custom on that day for the children of the village to parade from the old school to the church, preceded by the village band. They brought gifts of eggs and flowers for distribution to the hospitals of the district. There is no parade or band now, but the children still bring their gifts to the Feast Day Service. Previously a small fair would visit the village at that time and would stay for a week. The annual Garden Fete for the church took place at that time and people used to hold parties in their homes, when they enjoyed home-cured stuffed chine.

A new school has now been built at the east end of the village. Apart from the Five Bells, the other two pubs in the village are the King's Head and the Lord Nelson.

At the Brickyards, down Hacconby Lane, there is a field where years ago bricks were made. When the present owner bought the field, about 30 years ago, one kiln was still there and several mounds where others had been, but it is thought that it is over 100 years since bricks were made there. Bricks from these kilns were used in the building of a farm-house near the field.

Moulton 🐚

Moulton is a pleasant small village halfway between Holbeach and Spalding.

Its 800 year old church, All Saints, known as 'Queen of the Fens', has three fonts; an ancient stone one, an 'Adam and Eve' one and a Victorian one which dominates the view on entering the building. The rood screen too, is worthy of note as is the crocketed spire. The church's near neighbour, the eight-storey mill, is believed to be the tallest in England and can be seen from many miles distant.

The new vicarage in Church Lane just a short distance away, stands in the paddock adjoining the large old vicarage. There is a doctor's house opposite and many new director-type houses along the lane.

Facing the church across the village green is Harrox House, all that is left of the once popular Moulton grammar school. Founded in 1550 it closed, amalgamated with Spalding grammar school, in 1939. Only a small number of Old Boys remain but many are the tales they tell on Reunion Day on the nearest Saturday to 21st June every year! The village board school standing at the entrance to the playing field in Broad Lane is now a modern community centre well used by the many village clubs of all kinds.

The Swan is now the only public house still functioning. Not long ago there were five pubs in the village, the Bell and the George on the High Road, the Axe and Handsaw next to Harrox House and the Station Hotel. The old station buildings have become a thriving guest house which is very popular at Tulip Time.

In the short High Street leading from the church there is a post office-cum-newsagent's and confectioner's, a butcher's shop and a packing shed and large offices of JL Farms, part of Geest Industries. Finally the new medical centre staffed by three doctors with nurses and dispensers is a very welcome addition to village amenities. Across the road a grocer's-cum-general shop stands next to the Swan together with a ladies' hairdresser's shop, a ladies' and gentlemens' hairdresser's and a newly opened video library.

High Street joins Station Road at Cobgate corner where there are pensioners' bungalows and other council houses as well as many private houses with more being built all the time.

Leading from the village green to the High Road is Bell Lane, once lined on both sides with pink and white flowering chestnut trees. Now alas only a few remain. Instead even more houses and small estates have been built and the street are all named after masters at the grammar school. These are Harrox Road, Burnstone Gardens, Reynolds Gardens and Hatt Close.

At its north end Bell Lane joins the busy High Road where Park House stands in parkland, the only open space left in the village. The old Bell Inn which stood opposite Park House has been replaced with new houses. The only garage and petrol station in the village is also here.

Navenby 🐌

One of the string of villages along the A607 Lincoln to Grantham road, Navenby stands high on the Cliff, with excellent views down into the Brant valley.

The main High Street is a pleasant conservation area with listed buildings of stone, many of which have been restored in recent years. To the east of the village runs the Ermine Street, which was the pilgrims' way from York to Canterbury. Around this area relics and coins from the Roman era have been found, which makes it evident a Roman settlement may have been the beginning of this community.

As long ago as 1221 Navenby was granted a charter to hold a fair and markets, and in recent years a carnival was organised to revive this right. Agriculture has always played an important part in the area, especially in the Middle Ages, when the village had a weekly market around the butter cross on the village green. Today no one can remember the village cross and the fairs, and gone are the old village craftsmen, the wheelwright, blacksmith, saddler, cobbler, tailors, threshers, carriers and fire brigade. Today Navenby is fortunate to welcome two new businesses into the village, a glass engraving shop and an art gallery.

The village lost its railway station in the early 1960s. The old village school which was built by subscription on the site of the pinfold, has recently been made into a private dwelling. A new school along with a village hall was built in East Road in 1976, catering for children from neighbouring villages.

At the beginning of the century there were six public houses, but today there are only three, one of which is the Lion & Royal Hotel which has the Prince of Wales feathers displayed over the front door. This was presented by Edward VII, Prince of Wales when he stopped to change his clothes after hunting in 1870. A brass plate bearing the inscription 'In this room HRH Prince of Wales changed his clothes' can be seen in one of the bedrooms!

As early as 1857 Navenby had its own gas works, but all that remains today is the name of the lane. The church of St Peter is chiefly 14th century (the nave earlier than the chancel), but the north-west pillar of the five nave arcades (more massive than the rest) has stood since about 1180. On the north side of the sanctuary is the Easter Sepulchre, being one of two within the county of Lincolnshire. The western tower has six bells, which are still rung for services today.

Navenby is very self contained and has most amenities, which include a local bakery, butcher, grocer, fish shop, newsagent, village post office, garden shop, pet stores, hairdresser, freezer centre, antiques, Chinese take away, undertaker and restaurant. Two doctors run a practice in the village for Navenby and surrounding villages. A large development of properties has recently been built, which has attracted families from other parts of the country. Plans for even bigger estates are being discussed, to be incorporated in the area in the near future.

Nettleham 🌿

Nettleham is a large village lying three miles north of Lincoln. The centre of the village is designated as a conservation area. There is visual evidence of Nettleham's long history alongside the Methodist chapel, where large grassy mounds mark the site of the 11th century Bishop's Palace, an ancient monument of national importance and yet to be fully explored.

The traditional green forms one of the main focal points in the village and proudly displays a village sign, a recent attraction, a traditional red phone box, two 'Best Kept Village' signs, a war memorial and many trees of varying ages. Many of the stone cottages around the green and on the High Street date from the 16th, 17th, 18th and 19th centuries and are listed buildings. The street around the green bustles with activity as this accommodates most of the shops and also leads to the health centre and public library.

The parish church, a listed building rebuilt in 1891, exhibits work of the 13th, 14th and 15th centuries. It stands in a pleasant setting of trees and by its side is a quiet, natural area with seats and footpaths. It is approached from the High Street by way of a footbridge over the beck which flows through the village. The beck runs alongside the road in the vicinity of the church and then a footpath provides a pleasant waterside walk and a home for nearly 100 mallard ducks. There are many attractive public 'right of way' walks and a plan of these is to be found in the library.

The former primary Church school, also a listed building, provides a venue for the social services, Age Concern, the youth club and many village activities. The village hall is built on one of the new housing estates and can seat 200 people. The village can also boast a very large sports complex named after its twinned French village, Mulsanne. The children too have a playing field.

In recent years the Lincolnshire Police Headquarters has been built on the outskirts of Nettleham, adjacent to the A46 road.

Nettleham has assumed a dormitory function for Lincoln and many of the 3,200 residents work in the city. Property is very much sought after and Nettleham is considered to be one of the best villages in which to live.

Normanby le Wold 🐝

This small enclosed village with no through road, lies near the highest point of the Lincolnshire Wolds, some 543ft above sea level.

The church was largely restored in the Victorian era, but the tower is around 700 years old and the arches of the nave are 13th century. There is a curious corbel on the arch spanning the old south aisle, a carving of a man apparently in the throes of toothache, one hand raised to his head, the other holding his mouth wide open. There is also a fine medieval font like a pillar, enriched with a double band of quatrefoils and wavy pattern.

The church at the north-east is sheltered by some fine old beech and chestnut trees but the south side is exposed to the wind and rain from the prevailing south-west winds, and looks over the intervening valley to Walesby and the old church on the neighbouring hill.

There are approximately twelve households within the vicinity of the church and a further half dozen or so on outlying farms.

In recent years a walk, part of the Viking Way, has become popular and its route passes within a few feet of the church tower, leading across fields at the top of the cliff and then steeply descending to the village of Walesby. The road into the village from Nettleton top commands magnificent views across the great Lincoln plain to the towers of Lincoln Cathedral and castle, and on a fine day the cooling towers of the Trent valley can be clearly seen.

North Kelsey 🐚

North Kelsey lies just inside the Lincolnshire border. It has a long history and is mentioned in the Domesday Book of 1086, when it was called Norchelsie.

Whilst there has been a considerable amount of house building in the village recently, it has been mostly infill building and the village is still, in the main, its original size. The main High Street zigzags its way through the village with a myriad assortment of little winding roads leading off it. In the centre of the village there is a triangular village green with a recently restored pump to one side. This is known as the Bywell. There is a story that the water has magical powers and whoever drinks it has no desire to leave the village. Within living memory strings of farm carts with water barrels would line up to get their water supply for the steam threshing machines used during the harvest.

All Hallows' church is built of local stone, a gingery brown in colour, very worn and weathered with a small squat square Norman tower. Two buildings of note are next to the church, the manor house and Church Farm. The manor house is built in traditional style and Church Farm is a striking black and white building. The first recording of a vicar was in 1276 but there was possibly an earlier church.

Very little building before the 18th century is visible in the village but there is an extensive historical and archaeological background. There are strong links to Roman times, two sites of Roman villas are known in the village. Much information can be gained from the Rev A. Kerswill's book *North Kelsey, a brief history*.

Most of the village was owned by the Nelthorpe family of Scawby in South Humberside but in 1867 there was a great auction in Brigg, when much of the property was sold.

If you look carefully round the village you can trace a particular style of brick decoration on some of the older houses which is also to be seen on the older houses in Scawby. The decoration takes the form of rows of contrasting coloured brick triangles on the roof edges of the gable ends of the houses.

There have been three schools in the village in the last hundred years. The oldest school building is used as the local Community Association hall. The school in the centre of the village in School Lane is at present empty and is to be disposed of. The newest primary school building was officially opened in 1988 and provides a valuable meeting place for Women's Institute meetings, adult education classes etc.

There are two public houses in the village, the Royal Oak which is close to the village green and the Butcher's Arms at the end of Middle Street. Diagonally opposite from the Butcher's Arms is a property called The Beeches. This is house of character with a large area of ornamental water and some fine old trees.

There is in the village a sports club which comprises a tennis club and a bowls club. There is a sandpit next to the bowling green, the sand being of very fine quality and used for specialist work. In the sandpit there is a trace of a coral reef, left from the time aeons ago when North Kelsey was a coral island! This was in the time when there was a stagnant inland sea at nearby Greetwell.

There is a strong farming tradition in the village with associated trades. The Cherry Valley Duck Farm offers work to many, as do the nearby steel works in Scunthorpe.

Whilst there are few remarkable buildings in North Kelsey there are many remarkable people. Native born villagers with very long memories are fascinating to listen to, and there is a strong link with the arts with many painters, sculptors and needlewomen. Longevity appears to be a North Kelsey trait, nonagenarians are not rare.

So, what is North Kelsey? A pleasant but unremarkable place to walk through but an ideal place to live, peaceful, calm and friendly.

Northorpe

Northorpe is a small village which, with the adjacent deserted village of Southorpe, lies about six miles north-east of Gainsborough.

Most of the population of about 140 live around the church, which is dedicated to St John the Baptist and stands on a slight rise. The church dates from the 12th century and services are still held every Sunday morning at 8.30am. Beside the church is the Old Vicarage built in 1877, now a private home.

The village also has a Methodist chapel to which all are welcomed at 10.30am for the Sunday service.

The old manor house or Hall originated in the 16th century and is now a ruin. The present Northorpe Hall was built around 1875 and is now an hotel and restaurant.

Of the original farms, Manor Farmhouse and Charity Farmhouse probably both date from the late 17th century. Cold Harbour Farm lies just outside the village. This name, which is quite common, is thought

116

by some to refer to ancient Roman buildings and Roman coins have been found in a field within the village.

Low Farmhouse has been demolished recently but Parkside Farm on the outskirts has a large herd of prize-winning South Devon cattle. It is also the centre for a number of rare breeds of cattle, sheep, goats and pigs. These can be viewed by arrangement.

The old schoolhouse, built in 1846, is now the village hall. There is a playing field for children in the centre of the village.

This is a quiet village with no industry other than the hotel/restaurant and farming. Public transport is virtually non-existent.

North Owersby

Owersby covers a large area from the busy A46 in the east to the quiet river Ancholme in the west, with the village of North Owersby lying roughly in the centre: the hamlet of South Owersby, now only a farm and four adjacent houses lies about half a mile to the south.

North Owersby, mentioned in the Domesday Book when it was known as Aresbi, was for several hundred years an estate village, owned at one time by the Monson family of nearby South Kelsey, and later by the Angerstein family from Norfolk, before the estate was dispersed in the early years of this century.

Many of the old houses were built from the local yellow Owersby bricks, though the vicarage and a few other houses were of red bricks. Apart from 20 council houses built just before and after the Second World War, there has been practically no new development from the 1920s to the 1980s, since when several new houses have appeared. The church of St Martin, which stands on the highest point of the village, dates from medieval times though it was restored in 1888. It is now the only place of worship, though three former chapels can be seen within the village. One of these houses the post office cum general stores. The school, dating from 1705 when a local shoemaker left £80 for the education of twelve poor children of Owersby, closed in 1977. It has been converted into a house, but the old bell tower still remains.

Although agriculture is the main business of the area, there is a busy woodyard between North and South Owersby and in the village what was once the blacksmith's shop now makes machinery for the food processing industry.

Next to the blacksmith's shop is the old village pump and a replica of the village stocks put there in 1987 by the Parish Council, a harmonious blending of the old and the new into a pleasing whole, as is all of Owersby, both North and South.

North Somercotes

The village got its name from the reclaimed land on the coast originally called salt pans, which was turned into good grazing land. During the summer farmers from the Wolds brought their sheep down to graze, hence the name 'summer lots', being an old word for fields.

During the Second World War the RAF established a camp at Donna Nook, part of the village which borders the coastline and which was later used as a prisoner of war camp. This site is still used as a bombing range for planes from many parts of the world.

Along this part of the coast was a pack horse trail, starting at Tetney Haven and with a stop for refreshment at the old pub The Ark, which was nearly on the sea bank. For many years the lifeboat was launched at Donna Nook manned by a local crew. The coastguards still have a lookout on top of the dunes.

North Somercotes Church

It is understood that this village was a favourite haunt for smugglers. The road known as Warren Road was the original sea bank. On this road is Locksley Hall which has an association with Tennyson. The present village is well served with many shops, garages, three pubs, a Methodist church and the parish church of St Mary, which dates from the 13th century. There is a resident dentist, modern health clinic with three doctors, a men's billiard and snooker hall, a thriving Women's Institute and a well attended over 60s club. The village also has a senior High School and primary school, two play schools, a church hall and a village hall. The village has its own very active fire brigade.

A holiday camp built on the former gravel pit is a venue for many hundreds of visitors during the summer. This is bordered on all sides by a forest of trees.

The village has one of the best playing fields in the area, providing for bowls, tennis, football and cricket. The money for the upkeep chiefly comes from the annual carnival.

North Thoresby

North Thoresby is a village in the north-east corner of Lincolnshire of some 1,000 inhabitants, eight miles south of Grimsby. It is situated between the Wolds and the marsh, on the ancient Roman salt roads, the salt pans being situated nearer the coast. It includes the deserted medieval village of Autby. It was the last village to summer graze its cattle on the marsh before the marsh was drained and cultivated.

Today it is a pleasant village with two inns, a modern school, a church, St Helen's, and a chapel.

The dedication of the church to St Helen could mean that a Christian community has lived on this site for some 1,000 years and indeed there is evidence to corroborate this in the fragment of the Saxon cross now inside the church.

The chapel, with school attached, was built in the middle of the 19th century. The school has now been moved to more modern premises and the old school and school house have been modernised and refurbished to make a very welcome community centre known as the Wesley Centre. The refurbishing has been done in such a way that many of the features of the old school have been retained.

The new school stands on land that was part of the old westfield before enclosure and the land adjoins a playing field and allotments belonging to the Mapletoft Trust. The trust, set up in the mid 17th century, endowed a school for North Thoresby children, which flourished until 1899. The trust is now used to provide grants to local youngsters for further educational needs.

House names and street names reflect the ancient names of fields in some instances, in others the names of previous owners or occupiers of houses and land. Around the centre of the village are many older houses. Crispin Cottage bears the date 1761 on its lintel, the butcher's shop and adjoining houses are built of local stock brick, the Quality Foods shop is possibly Georgian, and the adjoining buildings in Church Lane are where a bakery once stood. The present buildings are old and tie bars have had to be used to prevent walls from bulging outwards. The tithe barn in Church Lane, adjoining the rectory and now a private residence, was once joined to the rectory and of course is where the tithe or tenth of every farmer's harvest was stored as the due of the rector. There were at one time a number of mills in the village, the sites of which are known and of course the railway, about a mile from the centre of the village. Many people enjoy a walk along the old track.

Today the village has all the amenities necessary for a self contained community. There is a post office, do-it-yourself shop, bakery, a butcher's and a hairdresser's together with three general grocery and newsagent's shops, and a bus service for travel to Louth and Grimsby.

The village hall, which has a memorial tablet to those villagers who fell in the First and Second World Wars, was opened in 1929 and renovated and extended more recently. There is a cricket pitch in the village, North Thoresby having had a cricket club at least since 1880, also a football field.

The village has been transformed since the 1960s by the building of new houses but it has managed to retain its character.

Old Bolingbroke

Lying in a dip of the Wolds, Old Bolingbroke is one of the most peaceful villages in Lincolnshire. Far from any main road, its present air of quiet calm must be very different from the days when it was an important market.

The reason for its medieval prosperity is indicated by the grassy foundations of Bolingbroke Castle, lying on the outskirts of the village. Built about 1220, it passed via various marriages into the hands of the House of Lancaster, and thus to the famous John of Gaunt, fourth son of Edward III and brother of the Black Prince. After his brother's death John of Gaunt became Regent of England on behalf of his young nephew – the ill-fated Richard II. In Bolingbroke Castle was born John's son, Henry of Bolingbroke, who later took the throne from his cousin Richard, and became Henry IV.

The castle eventually ceased to be a residence, but became an administrative centre for the Duchy of Lancaster and then gradually began to decay, probably because no-one of enough importance lived in it to justify extensive repairs.

But it was during the Civil War that the castle finally became 'one of the ruins that Cromwell knocked about a bit'. Bolingbroke was a Royalist stronghold and in 1643 it held out against a siege by Parliamentary troops from Horncastle until the Royalists were defeated at the nearby battle of Winceby. Subsequently the castle was systematically demolished by order of the Parliamentary authorities and much of the stone was removed by the villagers to build their own houses.

At present the remains of the castle are slowly being excavated and restored, which makes return journeys to the site very worthwhile.

In a triangular plot outside the village church stands a sign bearing the arms of the Duchy of Lancaster, and planted all around it are roses of Provins, a gift from France to commemorate the association of the Duchy to that town.

The village church of St Peter and St Paul was unluckily sited too near the castle for its own good. Built about 1363 it was originally three times its present size, but during the siege and attack on the castle in 1643 the church was so badly damaged that only the south aisle remained. After the Restoration of the Monarchy this aisle and what was left of the tower were patched up to make a serviceable village church with rather odd proportions.

The village houses are of every variety of shape, size and design, from cottage to manor house, and include the mill house, now a private residence, and the village pub, the Black Horse. Among the few 'modern' buildings is the excellent village hall, which is used for a variety of functions.

Old Leake 🌿

The parish of Old Leake is about eight miles north-east of Boston on the A52 road. It is surrounded by three villages, Leverton, Sibsey and Wrangle, with the sea at the narrowest end of the village. The Hobhole Drain is almost a boundary line between Old Leake and Sibsey. This drain starts at Toynton St Peters and empties into the sea at Fishtoft.

There is a pumping station at East Fen which helps to control the flow of water to the next pump. The first pumping station used coal and steam, and the chimney is still a landmark in the wide expanse of fen country.

In the Domesday Book the spelling of the village name is 'Leche', meaning a watery, marshy place. Over the years much work has been done to drain more land.

As one goes to the sea, there is an old sea bank. Beyond that more land has been reclaimed with the newest bank for protection. Keeping the marshes and creeks in check, sea lavender and many other sea plants grow, along with the well-known samphire, which is still collected in season by a few hardy locals. To actually reach the sea, one has a long walk, so if you would like cockles for tea, remember to take your rake, bucket and a strong back since cockles are heavy to carry all the way home again! The cockles must be washed well and dropped into boiling water to cook. When fit, drained and washed in cold water, and shelled, they are worth all the effort.

Much of the local employment was, and still is, farming. Over the years this has changed from mixed dairy and arable, to mainly arable. The Lincolnshire potato is strong evidence of the land's fertility, along with a wide range of green vegetables and cereals.

There is St Mary's church (Anglican), dating from about the 1490s, and a Methodist church; a large secondary school (Giles), primary school, health centre, three public houses and a community centre – all of which serve Old Leake and the surrounding area.

In 1941 or 1942 a bomb fell on the school at Church End during the night, demolishing the building. When the children arrived at school the following day, they were re-housed – infants in the church and older children in a large chicken hut and the White Hart pub clubroom. The site was cleared and a new wooden school was erected, which was used until 1973.

The village is proud of its community centre (built in 1981), with all its amenities for the various activities that take place. Outside is a large playing field for football and cricket. The children have an area with swings, slides, etc.

The elderly are catered for with bungalows and a warden-controlled block of flats.

A magnificent row of elm trees (approximately 100 years old) were lost to Dutch elm disease; these trees have been replaced on the original site by St Mary's church, with a variety of trees which, in time, the children and grandchildren of the village will be able to enjoy.

Osbournby 🐑

Osbournby, or Osberneby as it was recorded in the Domesday Book, is situated on the A15, six miles south of Sleaford. It has a population of 250.

The manor once belonged to the Hussey family. In 1486 John Hussey fought in the battle of Stoke on the side of Henry VII and in 1509 was given large tracts of land in Lincolnshire. In 1537, having been accused and found guilty of taking part in a rebellion in Lincolnshire, he was executed at Tyburn. The Carr family bought the estate from the Husseys, and they brought sheep farming to the area from Northumberland. In 1604 they founded the Carr's grammar school in Sleaford, still used today. After the Carrs, the Herveys took over and then the Whichcote family. The first Baron Whichcote was created in 1660 but when the eighth Baron died in 1949 the estate passed to Nicholas Plain, his nephew, who still owns Osbournby Hall, five farms and some cottages in the village.

The parish church of St Peter and St Paul is a large building dating from the reign of Edward III. It still retains many of the old pew ends, which are richly carved. The font is Norman, ornamented with pillars and arches. There is also a Methodist church in the village, dating from 1874.

The old school was built by the lord of the manor in 1848 but has now been sold to private business. A new primary school is to be built to serve the surrounding area.

The village has a post office, general dealer, a newsagent and butcher. Bus travel is available to Sleaford and Grantham. The pub, the Whichcote Arms, takes its name from the local family and is situated on the A15, as is the village hall.

Pinchbeck 🐝

The word 'pinchbeck' in English dictionaries means a copper and zinc alloy used in cheap jewellery, which was introduced by Christopher Pinchbeck, a London watchmaker who originated from this village. Pinchbeck is situated two miles from Spalding on the busy A16 road and though the railway runs through the district there is no longer a station.

Records of the settlement go back hundreds of years and there was probably a wooden Saxon church in existence before the Norman Conquest. There is evidence that a Norman church was built about 1070 on the present site of St Mary's parish church and later an Early English church was erected on the Norman foundations. The present chancel and chapel were built about 1350, the tower and south porch being added later. It is interesting to know that members of the Wayet family were vicars through succeeding generations for a period of 131 years. The Laxton family also have a remarkable record as sextons, the office being handed on from father to son for a period of 124 years from 1784 to 1908. Opposite the church stands a fine war memorial set in a tree-lined lawn.

At the other end of the village is the Baptist church. The first Baptist meeting place was established about 1840 and at one time Baptists were baptised in the river Glen, attracting crowds of spectators.

The main village street is Knight Street, so named because of honours conferred upon the local Ogle family. There was once a guildhall in Pinchbeck from which one road derives its name. Past amenities were the village pumps and pond, the latter used by horses to quench their thirst when passing to and from the farms where they were used for working the land.

There are now three public houses in the village, the Bell, the Ship and the Bull. Opposite the Bull are the stocks, a reminder of a past form of punishment.

At one time annual horse races were held in the village on the Sunday nearest 22nd June, but apparently the event developed into a rather rowdy affair and finally ceased about 1850. These days the Pinchbeck Carnival is held in June.

During the Spalding Tulip Parade week, Pinchbeck church holds its own flower festival in company with other local churches. During this period the church tower is open and from the top a wonderful bird's eye view of the area can be obtained.

The excellent primary school is housed in a modern building completed in 1968 and is surrounded by playgrounds and a large sports field. The old school building is now used as an Adult Education centre.

The old village horse pond would certainly not be required these days as farms in the district are worked by a highly mechanised system. The main crops now are vegetables, sugar beet, cereals, daffodils, apples and soft fruit. Years ago flax was widely grown in the area and at one time there were 100 employees at the flaxmill.

Despite the large increase in the population Pinchbeck still retains its friendly, pleasant village atmosphere.

Rauceby

At the point where the Ancaster gap emerges into the fen areas around Sleaford lies the parish of North and South Rauceby, a mile apart, but sharing church, school, village hall and public house, with Rauceby Hall between. Rauceby is Danish in origin.

The Boon beck, which forms the boundary between the villages, feeds the lake in the Hall grounds. In 1791 the land was enclosed. North Rauceby was very largely owned by the Earl of Bristol, an absentee landlord, but there were 14 owners in South Rauceby.

After the Act, Adlard Welby Esq of Parhamdam in South Rauceby started to consolidate his estate, which he had inherited from his father and grandfather. Then, in 1842, he sold everything to Anthony Peacock Esq, who extended his holding in the village so that it became an estate village. He built, on the site of Parhamdam, an imposing residence, Rauceby Hall, designed by the architect William Burn. He created the lake and planted numerous trees. Mr Peacock, who changed his name later to Willson, rebuilt many of the cottages in the village, but there are a number still surviving which were built in the 17th and 18th centuries, all of stone and red pantiled roofs.

North Rauceby was little altered except for the vicarage and some of the farms until 1860 when Charles Kirk, an architect from Sleaford, built some new estate cottages for the Earl of Bristol. Since the Second World War a number of new houses have been built, mainly in South Rauceby.

The church has always been regarded as a focal point of village life and this is true of Rauceby. The church, mentioned in the Domesday Book, is dedicated to St Peter and has a tower and broach spire of the

13th century. During the 19th of 20th centuries, the church has been extensively repaired, with stained glass windows remaining as memorials to the Willson and other families.

The present village school was built in 1842 by subscription. The public house (The Bustard) replaced, in 1860, an older inn, the Robin Hood, which stood at the south gate to the park, and a reading room was replaced by the village hall which residents of both North and South Rauceby use for their leisure pursuits. The village still continues the tradition of a Harvest Supper and Garden Fete at the Hall.

Rauceby remains a desirable place to live, attractively set in beautiful established park and woodland. It is still essentially linked to the estate and Hall and is based on tradition and a sense of history. Residents of both villages are a part of one community.

Revesby

Situated on the A155 Sleaford to Skegness road, twelve miles north of Boston, Revesby village is a good example of 19th century architecture. It is a truly charming place with its tree-lined road and village green, where church, old vicarage and almshouses are grouped to form a compact nucleus for the village.

St Lawrence's church was built in 1891, to the design of C. Hodgson Fowler, by the Rt Hon Edward Stanhope and James Banks Stanhope. This church is successor to one built in 1700, which in turn succeeded a medieval church. Inside the church, round the walls of the sanctuary is panelling with carvings of trees, vines and ivy with mother of pearl inlay. One of the oldest things here is a transitional Norman shaft piscina, now used as a font. In the aisle is a monument to Joseph Banks Esq, who bought Revesby estate for £1,400 in 1714 and died in 1727. He built the earlier church and bequeathed the almshouses, since rebuilt. Also on the monument is an inscription to William Banks, father of Sir Joseph Banks the naturalist.

In the belfry is an aerial view of the site of the Cistercian abbey destroyed during the Dissolution of the Monasteries. The site of the abbey itself, now only grassy mounds, lies south of the village reached by a narrow shady lane. There is, however, a granite stone with an inscription placed on the site of the high altar.

About half a mile from the village green, through fine iron gates, can be glimpsed the creepered walls of the great house known as Revesby

Abbey. The Abbey, built of Ancaster stone in Elizabethan style was erected in 1845 by James Banks Stanhope.

A former owner of the estate was Sir Joseph Banks, who was President of the Royal Society from 1778 until his death. He encouraged voyages and travels of discovery, notably those made by Captain Cook. He was also a promotor of the gigantic undertaking of the drainage and enclosure of the Lincolnshire fens.

In the nearby village of Mareham-le-Fen in the church, is the tombstone of James Roberts, who in the years between 1768 and 1771 sailed round the world with Sir Joseph Banks and Captain Cook.

In Revesby Park fallow deer can be seen peacefully grazing. North of the park is a reservoir of 40 acres, a local beauty spot which provides visitors with woodland walks and the opportunity to see many species of wildfowl which frequent the area. Permission must be obtained from the Estate Office on the Boston Road, during office hours.

Each year Revesby holds a gymkhana on May Day. On the last Saturday in June there is a Folkday and an evening ceilidh, both on the village green. On the first Sunday in August there is a Country Fair in Revesby Park.

Five miles along the Horncastle road from Revesby is Scrivelsby Court, the ancient home of the Dymokes, hereditary Champions of England since 1350 (by virtue of their holding this manor). The 19th century house was demolished and the present one has been converted from the gatehouse of the older house. The lion gate (c1530) was rebuilt in the early 19th century. Humphrey Repton laid out the grounds before 1791, and there is a herd of fallow deer in the park.

Rigsby 🦌

A delightful village on the edge of the Wolds with long views to the coast, Rigsby has one large farmhouse and six smaller homes housing the present 14 inhabitants! A new house, modern, but in keeping with its surroundings, has recently been built on the site of an old condemned cottage. By its side a sty, home of many a fat pig, remains, protected by law, to tell its story of past rural life.

In the church of St James, built in 1865 to replace an earlier, burntdown, thatched one, there is a 500 year old font and a Norman arch. A medieval helmet and sword, hanging near, take one's thoughts back to the days when the parish was of much importance and Gilbert of

Rigsby was lord of the manor. A report of his judicial court records that one parishioner, who committed the offence of not sweeping his causey (causeway) was in mercy of the lord, fined two pence – not then the paltry sum it is today. A service is held in the church once a month and, very rarely, a wedding or funeral of some one with past connections takes place.

The adjoining hamlet of Ailby has a charming, low, thatched farmhouse, three or four cottages and ten inhabitants.

Two maintained footpaths link Rigsby, Ailby and Alford.

Rigsby Wood has been for some years a nature reserve and now is of great interest to visitors on open days.

Rippingale ꒒ꆤ

In the District of South Kesteven in Lincolnshire lies the village of Rippingale. It is situated so that to the east lies the flat landscape of the fens of East Anglia while immediately to the west, undulating terrain and large wooded areas are to be found. No trunk roads pass through the village though the A15 passes within a quarter of a mile – south to Bourne and Peterborough and north to Sleaford and Lincoln.

Present day Rippingale is a pleasant village with some 650 residents. Some houses were built in the 19th century, with one or two in being from the 18th century, but there are many modern houses which have been built in place of former demolished properties and on spare land. There has been a policy of not extending the village boundary outwards and thus far this policy has been adhered to and the actual population has fluctuated little over some centuries.

The surrounding area is wholly agricultural except for the woods, the management of which is in the hands of the Forestry Commission.

The village presently has a Church of England primary school, educating some 70 pupils. It was built in 1856 but has been refurbished and enlarged whilst still keeping in character.

There is a fine pub – the Bull Inn, and the former manor house has become a residential hotel. Present amenities also include a fine village hall and two flourishing general stores, one incorporating the post office.

Rippingale is served by two churches. The Methodist chapel was built in the 1930s to replace the former Wesleyan chapel, which came into being in 1832 and is now a private residence. The parish church of St Andrew has stood in the centre of the village beside the village green for centuries. The porch is the oldest part of the present church and dates from the 12th century. The great tower was added in the 15th century and is a local landmark which can be seen for miles around.

The village playing field caters for football and tennis and has a children's play area, and there each year, in early July, the village feast is held.

The earliest historical mention of Rippingale is to be found in AD806. It was then spelled 'Riapencal' deriving its name from three syllables of Celtic origin – ri(upper), apen(river) and cal(forest). At that time the great forest of Kesteven was an extensive wooded area stretching 15 miles in length from Market Deeping to the north.

The village was granted a charter in 1268 to hold a fair and a market – a stone column still stands on the village green and this is thought to be the remains of the village cross erected at that time.

Stories of Rippingale characters are legend – one of the most notable is Ann Hardy, who was born and died here and is buried in an unmarked grave in the churchyard. She was the tallest woman in Britain, being 7 ft 2 inches when she died at the age of 16.

In the 14th century, the parish priest alleged that a wooden statue known as 'Jurdens Cross' which 'stood in certain fields within the parish bounds near the high road' had worked miracles. Bishop Buckingham of Lincoln believed that this was a money making exercise and came out strongly against it in 1387 but in 1390, the Pope granted a licence to the rector to build a chapel on the spot to attract pilgrims, and to hold services there. The chapel apparently survived as a hermitage into the 15th century but no further miracles are known to have taken place.

Ropsley

Ropsley is situated six miles to the east of Grantham. It is the birthplace of Richard Fox, Bishop of Winchester, who founded the King's School in Grantham, a grammar school in Taunton and Corpus Christi College in Oxford. He was born in 1448 at the Peacock Inn (a stone cottage which still stands on High Street) and died in 1528. The village pub named the Fox's Brush is however not thought to have been named after him, but after the animal.

The church of St Peter dates back to the 12th century and its eight-sided spire houses two bells (one now cracked) and a clock. The font dates back to the 15th century. Local quarries provided stone for the building and local timber was used to span the roof. A Norman window is still in existence in the south wall of the chancel and seats for the clergy cut into the stonework can still be seen there. The church register shows entries dating back to 1558.

The original school, with a house for the master, was built in 1717 by James Thompson and rebuilt in 1846. The present school building dates back to 1874. There still stands a fine bell tower, housing a usable bell, which is also depicted on the school badge.

Eight old people's bungalows now replace Tylers Row on Grantham Road, which comprised two sets of four cottages. 'Well Yard' was close by, but the deep well has recently been filled in.

One shop now exists, housing the post office at the rear. Present day life in the village is very different from the days when it was unnecessary for anyone to shop beyond the local streets. You could buy meat, groceries, or bread, employ the shoemaker, tailor or use the services of the carrier who visited regularly with his large horse-drawn van. Even as late as 1937 there were two bakers, two shopkeepers, two grocers, a miller, motor engineer, dairyman, physician, wheelwright, joiner, saddler, tailor, bootmaker and three butchers all trading in the village. Now only a handful of people still work in the village on the five farms.

Ruskington 🐿️

Ruskington is 16 miles south of Lincoln on the 'old way of the towns' formerly used by hawkers, which passes through 13 villages between Sleaford and Lincoln. White's 1856 directory describes it as a large village upon a plain, with a fine stream of water running through it. It is now one of the largest villages in the county with a very long history. A prehistoric route from the Wolds to the Ancaster Gap which passed through the present parish is known, as well as the line of a Roman road seen in aerial photographs.

An Anglo Saxon burial ground of the 6th and 7th centuries was discovered in 1871 and has been partially excavated several times since. Some of the men were buried with their weapons beside them and the women with simple jewellery such as beads and brooches and other personal possessions.

The village appears in the Domesday Book of 1086 as Reschintone. At that time there were 38 families, three water mills, a church and a priest. The lord of the manor owned twelve teams of oxen. The later Norman church has had alterations and additions made down to the 19th century. The spire was never replaced after falling down 300 years ago. In 1566 the churchwardens reported that some handbells which belonged to the church in Queen Mary Tudor's time had gone 'wee knowe not howe'.

A map of 1758 shows the layout of the streets very similar to the present day, with the stocks for malefactors, a workhouse, tithe barn, a pound for stray animals, fords in the beck and an open sewer! The fords have been replaced by bridges but the beck is still there with ducks swimming on it, and daffodils planted by the children among the cherry trees. The beck has flooded many times into the High Street and it froze during a hard winter in the Second World War. There is an old saying that you are not a true Ruskingtonian until you have fallen in the beck.

During the Second World War army vehicles and guns were parked under the trees by the beck. Many troops were billeted in Ruskington, and a memorial in the church and a new road named Arnhem Avenue commemorate the soldiers who trained here and left to fight that famous battle. Those who never returned are still remembered at the annual reunion of veterans and a service in the parish church.

With a population of nearly 4,000, Ruskington is now a thriving community with a large animal foodstuffs mill, a modern meat products factory sending supplies to chain stores over a wide area, building firms and other small business concerns. Its proximity to several RAF stations has resulted in a growth of population and a corresponding rise in the variety of shops and businesses. One wonders what the Domesday Book surveyors would think of the building societies, estate agents, medical and dental facilities, fish and chip shops and the Chinese restaurant!

Saxilby-with-Ingleby 🐾

Saxilby-with-Ingleby, six miles north-west of Lincoln on the A57, twelve miles from Gainsborough, where you can arrive by car, bus, train or boat! The village population has grown from less than 400 in 1800 to almost 3,500 today.

The parish church on the northern edge of the village is dedicated to the Benedictine abbot St Botolph, great traveller and missionary. Built on the highest ground in the village, 57 ft about sea level, the oldest part of the church is the north aisle with its Norman door. The lofty Perpendicular style forms the remainder of the church. The tower, a copy of the original, was rebuilt in 1908 and dedicated by Bishop Edward King. It has a fine peal of six bells.

Before Saxulf and the Danes invaded, the Romans were very active in the area; coming to Saxilby by cruiser along the Foss Dyke canal you are following in their footsteps! They extended the use of the river Witham and Brayford Pool at Lincoln by digging the Foss Dyke to link with the river Trent at Torksey Lock, giving them trading access to the Midlands and Humber estuary. Today the canal-side (Bridge Street) is a hive of activity. In 1987 the Parish Council, West Lindsey District Council and British Waterways developed the south side of the canal, repairing the banks, forming picnic sites and conservation areas, and providing riverside walks and seats. A former railway footbridge, from Claypole, crosses the water giving easy access to the moorings and other amenities. During the winter months the banks are lined with hardy anglers with brollies, rods and bait.

On Bridge Street, the Sun Inn is said to be haunted, having connections with the local murderer Tom Otter. A local poacher/labourer, he married his wife Mary in 1806, then murdered her the same day. After the trial and execution his body was hung from a gibbet in Tom Otter's Lane about one mile outside the village towards Drinsey Nook. The gibbet collapsed in 1850 and gibbet irons can be seen at Doddington Hall. The legend is that on the anniversary of the deadly deed, ghostly noises and movements are heard.

In 1935-6 a notable incident took place. The marchers from Jarrow to Parliament on the desperate trek to save their shipyards, stayed a night in Saxilby. It is a memory of childhood that has stayed with villagers. The weary exhausted men, with worn out clothes and boots and tired faces congregated between the public houses, the Ship and the Sun. The ladies of the village fed them and provided blankets and water to wash in the 'White City', a large building used for a multitude of gatherings situated where now the car park of the Ship is. The two shoe repairers mended their boots and they were sent on their way in the morning with food and warm wishes.

A ten minute train ride from Lincoln brings you to Saxilby, where until recently the Victorian station was active; this building is no longer in use, and the large engine shed occupied land where new properties now stand. Leaving Station Yard on your right you see Saxilby Youth Club, which until 1968 was St Andrew's church, a mission church of St Botolph's.

Further along High Street, outside Walnut House is the village sign, showing the church, a poacher, a sailing barge, and the head of a Lincoln Red cow. This was erected in 1984 in memory of Councillor Geoffrey Ford.

The village hall was once one of four chapels in the village. Greatly extended in 1975 it is now home for a host of village activities. Next door to the hall, architects occupy the old infant school built in 1871 and further along there is Saxilby Riding School. Across the road is the new Methodist church built in 1940, set amidst neat rose gardens.

Saxilby has been known world-wide as the home of Rose Bearings, whose products are used in the space industry, racing cars and Concorde. Expansion has meant a move to Lincoln. L & K Fertilizers-Kemira Ltd find their way to all parts of the country and overseas.

Few ancient houses are left in the village, but the black and white half-timbered cottage in the High Street built in the 16th century is reputed to be a cruck-frame dwelling. The Manor House, Church Road has roof timbers of the same century. The National school built in 1845 next to the parish church, has been converted into a house, with its main features still visible. New residential estates in the centre of Saxilby have some most attractive gardens.

Scamblesby 🦊

The village nestles in a valley of the Lincolnshire Wolds, designated by the Department of the Environment as an area of Outstanding Natural Beauty, mid-way between Louth and Horncastle.

Agriculture is the main industry, the acreage amounting to 2,002 acres, and the chief landowners being the Church Commissioners.

The population is made up of various professions, trades, the farming fraternity and retired people.

The village is very fortunate to have a junior and infants school, with an excellent staff committed to the welfare and well-being of the pupils, together with a Parent Teachers Association; a village shop and sub-post office, a village hall and a public house.

The Parish Council is responsible for affairs of local government, the parish of Cawkwell now incorporated with Scamblesby.

The County mobile library service is a great asset to the village. A taxi service is available, the Royal Mail Post Bus service was commenced in 1960 and the Viking Way (which passes through the village) was opened in 1976.

The Methodist church was built in 1835, and extended in 1868. A new church was built on the site in 1977 and the official opening took place in January 1978.

St Martin's church is built of stone with chancel, nave and a turret containing one bell; the register dates from 1569. The font has a massive and unusual bowl, and there are 18 bench ends, with faces peeping from fleur-de-lys poppy heads.

Scotter 🖑

Scotter is the largest village in the north of Lincolnshire and is located on land which slopes gently to the river Eau. It stands almost half way between Scunthorpe and Gainsborough and has a long history. Mention is made of Scotter in the Domesday Book (1086) and ecclesiastical records reveal that in 1190 King Richard I granted the right to hold a market and fairs. The reign of King John gave Scotter a confirmation charter and a visit from his Majesty in 1216. The King, trying to raise an army to repel the threatened French invasion, stayed in the inn facing the village green. The landlord of the inn, as a mark of honour to his visitor, redesigned his inn sign and incorporated the badge on the shield of the Officer in Charge – a sun and an anchor. The present hostelry stands on the same site and the 'Sun and Anchor' is thought to be unique among inn names.

The present manor house is a listed building, as is the old manor. The latter is situated across the river Eau from the church and it is said that underground passages connect the two buildings. Religion played an important part in the history of the village and St Peter's church occupies a prominent position overlooking the village centre. The history of St Peter's goes back to the 7th century. Above the present belfry door are the Ringers' Rules, in black and red Elizabethan lettering. Within the church there are copper and brass memorial plates dated 1599 and 1739. The village had three chapels also, only one of which has survived.

The main industries of Scotter have always been rural in nature and there is reference in historical records to three mills. One of these, in use until 1939, still stands. The Tower Mill was originally a post mill, built in the 15th century, and would have been essential to the agriculture of the surrounding area. Today's businesses relate to the service industries and there is a good variety of provision merchants, butchers, hairdressers, haulage etc. In the village there are also two public houses and one hotel.

Education in Scotter was the prerogative of a Church of England school until the old Lindsey County Council, in 1931, provided a new building, now housing junior and infant pupils. The former school is now used partly as a library and partly as a Youth Club.

Recreation is, in the main, provided for at the village playing fields. Football, cricket and tennis is played regularly throughout the year and a new bowling green is to be opened shortly. A splendid new village hall caters for indoor activities and meetings. A total of 21 organisations use the village hall at some time or another.

One of the more widely known of Scotter's activities is its Silver Band, which provides entertainment over a wide area. It also takes part in competitions with some success. The truly rural character of our village can be seen on a pleasant Sunday evening in the summer when the band plays to a gathering on the riverside.

Scotton

Scotton is a village of some 500 people and quite compact, in that it is only about a mile round what amounts to the perimeter road. A further 60-70 people live in a dozen houses and a nursing and rest home on the A159 Gainsborough Road which lie within the parish of Scotton. Its nearest neighbours are each about a mile away at Northorpe and Scotter, separated by arable fields only, because although thoroughly rural, the land is generally deemed too good for animal husbandry. Only the occasional flock of sheep is seen, mainly in spring, when their lambs are eagerly awaited by passers-by.

The oldest building is the 13th century church of St Genewys. It is an attractive building which has had plenty of maintenance to keep it in a good state of repair. There are two pieces of very old statuary lying on plinths, but the stained glass in the windows is Victorian and later. A small window at the eastern end of the south aisle has an interesting picture of the church itself, and on the north wall, by the altar, is a representation of the patron saint, St Genewys, Bishop of Clermont. The dedication of the church is not fully understood, but the present name, thought to be unique in the United Kingdom, goes back at least 200 years. Research has shown that Genewys (Genesius) was Bishop of Clermont Ferrand from AD 655 to AD 662, and being a good man and great philanthropist, has had his name commemorated in many villages and their streets all over France. There is considerable speculation as to why a relatively minor figure in French history should be the patron saint of a church in a tiny village in North Lincolnshire.

In the early 18th century the rector of Scotton, Dr John Morley, came to know the Wesley family in Epworth (a large village across the river Trent, standing on the Isle of Axholme). It was through the rector's patronage that the young John Wesley became a Fellow of Lincoln College, Oxford, and from that place worked on the spread of Methodism, with which the name Wesley is almost synonymous. Two Methodist chapels existed in Scotton, none survives; one was closed in 1969, and is now a private home in Crapple Lane. Another building which was changed into a home was the school in Eastgate which ran from 1880 to 1932.

In the village where most houses are post-1945, the pub is one of the very few old houses. It is the Three Horse Shoes, small but welcoming, having had a considerable re-fit in recent years, but not having its character spoilt. Almost next door is the shop/post office, by which there is the bus stop for the rather infrequent service.

A car is a necessity here, because the two main work and commercial centres are each about eight miles away at Scunthorpe and Gainsborough. In these days of mechanisation in farming, most working people commute to one of these towns which have heavy, light and service industries as well as their attendant offices. The closure of large parts of British Steel in Scunthorpe and the loss of heavy industry in Gainsborough meant that in quite recent times the area was very depressed. However, the vacuum left is being gradually filled with new developments bringing new opportunities for employment.

On the outskirts of the village proper there is Scotton Common, part of which is owned by the Lincolnshire Nature Trust. Within the boundaries of the reserve are rare plants and grasses, and many nesting birds. A permit is needed to make a visit.

Sibsey 🐚

Travellers along the A16 are following in the footsteps of prehistoric travellers along a sand and gravel ridge left by glaciers. Stretching from High Ferry, where it surfaces, to the Lincolnshire Wolds, this ridge connects the villages of Sibsey, Stickney and Stickford.

The original Sibsey was a Saxon settlement 'Siba-ey', the 'ey' meaning island so it was the Island of Siba. The island referred to cultivated land used for some grain and grazing, surrounded by wetlands which would have been dry in summer. Sibsey appears in the Domesday Book as Sibolci.

An example of Sibsey's rural history is the pinfold next to the A16 where stray cattle would have been impounded by the Pinder in the 18th century. He charged fines to the owners of the animals and had to pay double if his own animals were guilty! It is known that there were nearly 4,000 cattle and numerous sheep in the West Fen in the 1780s.

A feature of Sibsey is the Trader Mill, a six-sailed windmill in working order. People can see it in its full glory on open days each summer thanks to British Heritage. It was constructed in the 1870s from local clay bricks on the site of a previous post mill.

Nearby is 'The Trader', a local name for the Stonebridge Drain, a north to south watercourse running to Boston. It was built as a drainage channel at the beginning of the 19th century, and was formerly used by barges for farm produce and by a horse-drawn packet for passengers going to Boston market on Wednesdays and Saturdays.

The church of Saint Margaret is described by Pevsner as having 'a surprising interior'. It was built in stages probably on the site of a wooden Saxon structure. The central part of the church is oldest, being Norman, with Early English and Perpendicular additions.

In earlier times the village was a thriving community, self sufficient in every way. White's Directory of 1842 lists the professions of Sibsey residents which included a joiner, a plumber, a saddler, two farriers, three blacksmiths, seven boot and shoe makers, two cattle dealers, four bricklayers, three butchers, a draper and dressmaker, two millers and bakers, many publicans and a surgeon. More recently there have also been a builder and undertaker, a boatmaker, hairdressers, a coal depot in the station yard and a painter and decorator.

One local celebrity was Annie Besant, who was the wife of the vicar until she went to work in London late in the 19th century. As one of the

'Stocks Hill', Sibsey

first trades unionists she was a negotiator for the Matchgirls in their dispute in 1888 with their employers, Bryant and May.

Arthur Lucan, better known as Old Mother Riley on both stage and screen, was born in Sibsey in 1885 and lived in the village for many years.

Today the village facilities include a school for over 90 primary children, originally founded in 1723 by the vicar, a post office and stores, a chapel, a bowling green, three garages, two public houses, two ponds, a frozen foods shop, a machinery repairs service and a recreation field. The village is well served by rural rounds including a butcher, a fresh fish vendor and a greengrocer as well as the usual milk and postal deliveries. The railway station is no longer in service though trains do run along the line from Boston to Skegness.

The flat agricultural land around Sibsey is given over to arable production. The main cereal crop is wheat. Oil seed rape and vegetables such as peas, potatoes, sprouts and cabbages are also grown.

Although the attractive village of Sibsey was physically divided by the A16 trunk road in the mid 1970s, its unity comes from the friendliness of its people, for wherever a newcomer goes they are assured of a genuine welcome.

Skellingthorpe 🦆

About the time Lincoln Cathedral was being built, Skellingthorpe was a small hamlet on the high ground of the fen area west of Lincoln. Inhabitants either worked the land or made use of the many rabbit warrens which abounded on the poor soil. 'Skellingthorpe Duck' was said to be a London delicacy, so no doubt rabbits and ducks gave some people a meagre living.

Henry Stone was lord of the manor, who, lacking an heir, in 1693 bequeathed the land to Christ's Hospital, London. His coat of arms appears on the Stone Arms public house, which was in the area flooded to a depth of 6 ft when the Spalford bank burst in the 1700s. Farmers' wives travelled by boat to Lincoln market for three weeks until the waters subsided.

With the coming of day schools in the 1850s all landowners paid a tithe to the Spital Charity, which donated £50 for the 'poor and needy' of the parish. Nowadays a bible is traditionally given to every pupil leaving the village school from this fund.

In 1896 the railway arrived. The Great Central opened for passengers and goods traffic running from coast to coast. The 'goods' were mainly fish from Grimsby and coal from the Midlands. The station closed in September 1955 and the line completely closed in February 1980. The whole of the station site now belongs to the Parish Council. On it is built a community centre and a new youth hall. The old lamplighter's hut has been retained as a council store – but it still smells of paraffin!

Skellingthorpe was one of the largest parishes in England; the western boundary skirts the Nottinghamshire border and the 'Old Wood' is reputed to be the edge of Sherwood Forest. In the 1950s Lincoln City took over many acres east of the village, mainly the aerodrome which was built during the Second World War. The large Birchwood estate is now established there.

In 1982 the Women's Institute celebrated its Diamond Jubilee and to mark the occasion they presented the village with a pictorial oak sign, depicting various historical events, which was erected in the grounds of the community centre. The Parish Council have landscaped the immediate area to show it to best advantage.

Skellingthorpe is one of the fringe villages of Lincoln scheduled for 'growth', but those who live here intend to continue to strive to keep a village community.

Snarford 🐏

A scattered hamlet nine miles north of Lincoln, Snarford is notable for its church of St Lawrence, a stone building in Norman, Early Perpendicular and Decorated styles.

Inside are the wonderful tombs more reminiscent of a cathedral than a small church in a village where no evidence remains of any major residence. These are monuments to the St Pollor St Paule family. The earliest, 1582, is a canopied altar tomb bearing effigies to St Thomas St Poll and his wife. It is enriched by ten statuettes.

In a recess on the north wall and dated 1613 are two effigies representing Sir George St Poll, Kt and Bart, and Frances his wife, with their daughter Mattathia and weeping cherubs. Frances reappears as the Countess of Warwick on a round tablet with her second husband, Baron Robert Rich of Leize, Earl of Warwick, who died in 1618. On a Latin-inscribed wall plaque a former Snarford parson tells us that Frances initially married at 15 and after twelve years had a daughter Mattathia who died before her second birthday.

A further floor stone commemorates George Brownlow Doughty, 1743, who married a Lichborne heiress.

Snelland 🐏

Snelland, mentioned in the Domesday Book as Esnelant on Sneleslunt, lies three miles north-east of Langworth. The present population is 89. The original medieval village surrounded the church, but the only remaining traces are the uneven aspect of a grass field where old tracks and humps can be seen, particularly in wet weather. Also one ancient pasture retains the original ridge and furrow undisturbed. It is known as the Village Field. This ancient form of drainage still ensures the ground is rarely too wet for grazing and increases the acreage available.

The bridge over the beck, which runs through the village, is the only evidence of a former track. It can now be crossed when using one of the many footpaths leading from outlying farms and cottages to the village.

The railway opened in 1848 and this appears to have stimulated a rebuilding project in the village, much of which was owned by the Cust family. The station, built of Ancaster stone and closed in 1965, is now a private residence. Older villagers remember commuting to Lincoln and

Market Rasen and when the yards and field were full of cattle awaiting transport.

The blacksmith's house opposite the station was built in 1865, although the forge is older. The only industry in the village, apart from farming, the blacksmith is much sought after and works long hours. The carpenter's shop, a barn with outbuildings replacing a thatched cottage and buildings, was constructed in 1846 and the house in 1904. This is now a private house.

One barn, now two cottages, adjacent to the old track was built in 1850, while various farms were also built at this period. The Victorian wall letter box is still in use.

The rectory, built in 1862, is beside the church of All Saints, which was rebuilt in 1863 by the Cust family. It is in the early Decorated style and has a bell gable containing two bells. The key can be obtained from the blacksmith.

This century a small number of council houses and bungalows have been built, while older houses and cottages have been modernised and enlarged. At present Snelland is designated a conservation area where no expansion is visualised. The hamlet of Swinthorpe is a part of Snelland.

South Elkington

The small village of South Elkington (population about 200) is situated on the A631 Louth/Market Rasen road. It is in an area of mixed farmland, on the eastern edge of the Wolds, just two miles from the old market town of Louth.

Many of the buildings in the village date from Victorian times when the village centred around Elkington Hall. Buy an ice cream at the only shop, and wander up Church Lane to All Saints church. You will pass the war memorial, which dates the First World War as ending in 1919; the school, closed in 1984 and now converted into a house; and the Church Institute, an attractive timbered hall, given to the village by a former vicar, Canon J. G. Smythe in 1905, and used for various functions including WI meetings. Close by stands Park House, one of the two old vicarages in the village.

The 13th century chalk and stone church was restored during the 19th century. The chancel has a fine painted ceiling depicting the twelve apostles. In the well-kept graveyard, near the lychgate, grows an unusual thorny tree, the Honey Locust, planted to remind us of Christ's crown of thorns, and known as the Calvary Tree. It came from Palestine.

The site of Elkington Hall is reached by taking Back Lane. Built by the Smythe family, it was demolished in the 1970s, but many of the beautiful trees planted in the surrounding parkland still remain.

Elkington Vale is the old carriageway to the Hall and follows a wooded valley from the Lincoln Road. Along it are several magnificent Coast Redwoods, trees native to the Pacific coast of North America. They have done well in the comparatively dry Lincolnshire climate, and are home for many wood-boring creatures.

The whole area around South Elkington, despite being intensively farmed, is endowed with a network of footpaths. These are well-marked with signposts and waymarks, thanks to the co-operation between the LCC and the local landowner, C. B. Dobson. So don a pair of walking boots and discover the sights and sounds for yourself. The seasons provide an everchanging tapestry, with perhaps the colours of

The countryside at South Elkington

142

autumn or waving corn of summer being the most spectacular. Sporting activities give another dimension, fishing, scrambling, shooting, hunting and the annual Team Chase in Old Hall Park organised in the spring.

Nearer to Louth is Thorpe Hall which borders the road and has an interesting tale to tell. In Elizabethan days it was the home of Sir John Bolle, a knight who fought at Cadiz, where he won the affection of a Spanish princess. The story goes that she followed him home, but seeing him happy surrounded by his family, she died, and her ghost, 'The Green Lady', haunts Thorpe Hall and its grounds.

South Kyme 🐝

South Kyme stands on the river Slea, which flows through the flat Lincolnshire countryside. The fields now yielding a rich harvest of cereals and sugar beet once lay under water when the land was simply an undrained fen.

Kyme Eau, the waterway on either side of South Kyme, is home for leisure craft which pass by from the Witham Bottom lock, which has now been restored. A service is held once a year for the waterfolk, who tie up along the river side.

The 'Navigation' of the Slea can still be traced. Indeed you can't help but see the hump-backed bridge and the towpath which leads towards the church and tower, all that remains of the great castle which was built in the 14th century. It is said that a cow once rushed right up its stairs in fright. The moat and the fish ponds now stand dry, and are no longer used. It was thought at one time to have been the home of Robin Hood.

The village school is now a private residence, and only one shop remains, all the others long gone. Without a car in South Kyme you cannot go far because there are very few buses. There is only one public house in the village, named the Hume Arms.

People have lived askirt this fen since the earliest times known to man, and will continue to live here – even though the County Council map shows that South Kyme is under water!

Springthorpe 🌿

In the lovely old church, which dates from Norman times, in the village of Springthorpe, you may uncover a sad little tale about a young woman known as Mary Hill. She died on Shrove Tuesday 1814 when ringing one of the four bells. She was carried up to the roof and then fell to the floor hitting a large stone, this now forms the base of the font. In a glass case just inside the Norman doorway you will find the Maiden's crown. This is one of three carried at her funeral by three maidens dressed in white. They also carried three garlands and three white gloves. These garlands when carried at the funeral of any unmarried girl were a symbol of chastity. You will also find the framed story on silk, and the Maiden's poem.

The church claims an entry in the Domesday Book and the oldest part, the tower, is reputed to be Saxon. The nave is 14th century and the herringbone masonry in the south wall indicates that the work was carried out in the 11th century. There is proof of the existence of the parish of Springthorpe since this time, supplied by the list of rectors who held this living.

Included in the parish is the hamlet of Sturgate. This is a short walk from the village and you may want to return for refreshment in the New Inn!

Stewton 🌿

Stewton is a small village on the outskirts of Louth. It is totally agricultural and no building is allowed unless connected with agriculture.

It was once a busy village with village hall and active social calendar but this has now disappeared and all that now remains of the village is a very beautiful small but ancient church almost a thousand years old. St Andrew's is mostly Norman and consists very simply of a nave, a bellcote and chancel.

Stickford 🌿

There was a community in Stickford in the days of William the Conqueror. His surveyors for the Domesday Book probably approached it along a main road along the slightly higher belt of dry land separating the East and West Fens. There was a ford on this road, probably spanning a bit of swamp, and it is from this high road and ford that the village took its name, which they recorded as 'Stitchesforde'. The name suggests a village of Saxon origin, and the entry in the Domesday Book mentions domestic buildings and a church.

As far as is known, the oldest parts of the present parish church are early 13th century. These include the octagonal pillars of the south arcade of the nave; those of the north arcade are characteristic of the early 14th century, and there is a 13th and a 14th century window in the north aisle. Of special interest also are the medieval great bell (about 18 cwt) inscribed 'Sancte Gabriel' on the tower floor, the 15th century octagonal font with traces of painted decoration and the 15th century bench ends.

In 1349, the Black Death hit Stickford and parish records show that four vicars died of it that year.

There was a manor house until 1790, when it was destroyed by fire. All that remained were the stables which were converted into a house which is now called Manor Farm. Behind the farm there is a pond which is said to have been the fishpond of the manor house.

A thatched cottage on the main road was originally an estate cottage. It is thought to be 17th century or possibly earlier. A timber-framed 'mud-and-stud' building on the traditional central chimney longhouse pattern, it was later brick cladded.

In 1820, a tower mill was built, and ground corn until at least 1925. Stickford House was built in late Georgian times, and the vicarage in 1836.

Eleven acres of land were once occupied by paupers of the village and at Sutton, near Alford, a two and a half acre pasture was let for £5.10s.0d a year, the money being given to the poor. In the late 19th century and early this century needy people, sometimes numbering 40 or more, used to line up at the vicarage door to receive Christmas relief. Poor relief is still administered, but the identities of recipients are now confidential.

There is a drain through Stickford, known as Catchwater Drain. In 1856, a Stickford resident, George Bycroft, ran a packet boat between Stickford and Boston. It left Stickford at 7am on Wednesdays and Saturdays and returned at 3.30. He carried both passengers and goods and moored the boat at Bargate Bridge, Boston.

For many years, Isaac Hipkin and Son ran a large shop selling groceries, drapery and beer. They also sold coal, collected rates and kept cows. They owned teams of horses and travelled around Stickford and Stickford Fen selling provisions. Many customers, instead of paying cash for their goods, would barter for them with milk, eggs or butter. In the 1930s and 1940s there was also Smith's garage with a shop selling sweets, cigarettes and other small items and Wilson's, a baker's and confectioner's shop.

In the Second World War, although agriculture was a reserved occupation, many boys and some girls from the village joined the Armed Forces. Those at home were busy not only producing food but also training in the Home Guard and fire-watching. Lancasters were flown from nearby East Kirkby airfield, so there was considerable air activity. Bombs fell near the then church hall, which was a centre for whist drives, dances and concerts, but fortunately it was not hit.

Stickford still has a public meeting place, as the former school canteen is now run by a village committee as a community centre, and regularly used by the various organisations.

Stickney 🐑

Stickney is situated midway between Boston and Spilsby on the main A16 road. The church stands on a road junction beside the main road. It has a yew-shaded path up to the church door. The nave and base of the tower are 13th century with windows of 15th century work. A new tower was built at the beginning of this century and a resident of Stickney tells of his father conveying stone from Sibsey railway station to the church with his horse and cart. It stuck in his mind because once his father was backing the horse and cart to the workmen when the cartwheel ran over an old vaulted grave which immediately gave way and let the cartwheel drop into a hole in the ground. Despite such problems a fine tower was built with a good set of bells which can be heard today for weddings and calling people to worship on a Sunday. It is thrilling on a lovely summer's evening to hear the bellringers practising ringing the changes.

The railway was built through Stickney in about 1912. An old man used to tell of the times as a boy when he watched the workmen building it. He remembered one day when the Paymaster came to pay the construction men and he slipped in the mud. His case with the wages in fell open and the wages – gold sovereigns – fell into the mud. There was quite a struggle to find them and a few were lost. The local lads could be seen for some time afterwards scrambling in the mud to find a sovereign to take home.

The primary school stands near the church and teaches about 150 pupils. In the 16th century a gentleman called William Lovell left some money for Stickney to have a village school so when it was decided to build a secondary modern school in Stickney in 1959 it was named the William Lovell School in his memory. It has about 300 pupils, and stands further along the main road near to one of the two garages and a hairdresser.

There are two shops to provide for villagers' requirements, a post office combined grocer's store and a shop selling hardware, some clothes and groceries. The previous owner said he sold anything from a pin to an elephant. But it is doubtful that he was ever asked for an elephant!

On the main roadside amongst the houses and between the two schools is the doctor's surgery, in a building which was once the Plough Inn public house. Opposite is the one remaining pub, The Rising Sun. Many years ago the landlord upset a regular who told him, ' I hope your Sun never rises again'. The reverse happened: it remained open the longest.

Horbling Lane is a well populated lane off the main road with a fish and chip shop, the new rectory and many houses.

The road junction upon which the church stands leads through West Fen to Carrington. This road has many houses, a housing estate and two village halls together in one car park.

The old rectory is now a retirement home. The two windmills no longer work but one is the premises of a metal craftsman. A local farmer grows daffodils and his colourful fields cheer everyone in the springtime.

A short distance from the church towards Spilsby is the outdoor bowls club where excellent greens await the keen bowler. Residents like to congregate there on hot summer days to enjoy both the game and the company.

Close beside Stickney is the small parish of West Fen where there is an eight acre field of hills and hollows and a pit. The silt soil was taken from this field many years ago to repair the roads when carts and farm waggons left ruts, long before tarmacadamed roads were made. A reminder of the history of this field is the name of the farm, Silt Pit Farm.

Sturton by Stow 🐏

The old Roman road, Tillbridge Lane, runs through the village at the village green. Sturton is eight miles north-west of Lincoln.

There are several well preserved cottages in the village over 200 years old, notably on Tillbridge Lane. The Subscription Mill off Marton Road, a continuation of Tillbridge, was built in 1810. The old school-room on Tillbridge Lane was built in 1840. It is still in use for Parish Council and other meetings, and as a doctor's surgery.

St Mary's, Stow, is regarded as the 'Mother' of Lincoln Cathedral. It was built in Saxon times by the Bishops of Dorchester-on-Thames as a centre for the Church in Lincolnshire, and was endowed by Lady Godiva. After the Norman Conquest, when Lincoln acquired its own cathedral, St Mary's became simply a parish church (apart from a brief spell as a monastery). The church is cross-shaped, with a unique set of four huge Saxon arches around the crossing. The tower and its support-ing arches are 15th century, but the rest of the walls are almost all Norman or Saxon. A major restoration was done by J. L. Pearson (architect of Truro Cathedral) in the 19th century. This included the roof, the elaborate vaulting in the chancel, and many of the furnishings. The church also contains an ancient wall painting of Thomas a Becket, a 13th century font with pagan carvings, and a graffito of a Viking ship.

Although a much larger village, Sturton by Stow has never had its own parish church. But Pearson, while restoring St Mary's, Stow, designed a simple red brick mission church for Sturton, which was built in 1879. It is called St Hugh's, in honour of the Bishop of Lincoln who lived (and kept his pet swan) at nearby Stow Park.

Sturton by Stow was the first village in the county to have a Methodist Society in 1771, perhaps due to the fact that there was no established Anglican church in the village. John Wesley visited Sturton on 7th July 1779, possibly travelling via Tillbridge Lane from Horncastle, where he had preached the previous day. A notable early Methodist, Sarah Parrott, who lived at Bracebridge, walked every Sunday to join the Methodists, meeting in various homes. Methodism reached Lincoln via Sturton, mainly due to the efforts of Sarah Parrott. She invited a Mrs Fisher living at Gunnerby to live at Lincoln, which she did in 1788, and started up Methodism in Lincoln City. A plaque to Sarah Parrott can be seen in Sturton Methodist chapel, built in 1964, in the High Street.

St Edith's, Coates-by-Stow, is a tiny parish church in an isolated farmyard. The entire parish has a population of about 20. It is reached by going east from Stow (towards Ingham) for one and a half miles, then turning left. The church was built in Norman times, but is mainly late medieval (15th-16th century). It contains some unusual survivals from that period, including the stone altar slab, the pews and pulpit, and the carved chancel screen and rood loft. There are interesting 17th century memorials in brass and in alabaster, and the Royal Arms of Charles I is a rarity from the same age.

Sutton Bridge

The village of Sutton Bridge has many claims to fame, but it is not an ancient foundation as are many other villages in Lincolnshire. Many people only know it as a bottleneck on the A17 main road leading into Norfolk, but the swing bridge spanning the river Nene is the focal point of the village. It replaced the earlier one built by such eminent engineers as John Rennie and Robert Stephenson to provide main road and rail routes across what had been a dangerous two mile estuary. Certainly the members of King John's baggage train found it to be hazardous as it is said that the King's Treasure is still lying somewhere in the area. Perhaps that is why the local people are such keen gardeners, as they hope some day to find the treasure!

At the end of the 19th century the Midland and Great Northern Railway Company built the present swing bridge at a cost of £80,000 and it is unusual in being worked by hydraulic power. It was opened for

Cross Keys Swing Bridge, Sutton Bridge

traffic in 1897. The bridge, now a listed building, is in the process of being refurbished to deal with the traffic on the new bypass.

The main event in the history of Sutton Bridge was the construction of the docks, finished in May 1881, soon followed by their collapse the following month because of the shifting sands beneath their foundations. Over the years there have been many calls to revive the docks but this did not come to pass until 1988 when a new port was constructed. This is now expanding rapidly and will, no doubt, bring great changes to the life of the village.

Sutton Bridge has been associated with the RAF since 1926 when the first summer camp for airmen was opened. The flat and sparsely populated area was suitable for bombing and firing practice and it soon became a full-time Operational Training Unit. Villagers soon became used to seeing the Blenheims, Spitfires, Hurricanes, Wellingtons and many other types of aircraft in the wide fenland skies of this area. Many Battle of Britain pilots trained here. It was inevitable, therefore, for some of its complement to be killed during their stay at the station and many of them are buried in the village churchyard along with some local lads who were killed elsewhere and brought home for burial.

In the village church of St Matthew the altar in the north aisle was dedicated to their memory and a tablet of oak carries all their names. The altar frontal has the Service Crests of all the Air Forces commemorated.

Pilot training ceased in 1946 but a part of the aerodrome later housed a private landing strip from which private flying continued for some time.

Other landmarks on the outskirts of the village are the two lighthouses flanking the river Nene. In the late 1920s Sir Peter Scott, the famous Director of Slimbridge Wildfowl Trust and one of the great nature conservationists of our time, lived in the East Bank Lighthouse. At that time it was much nearer the sea as the land reclamation schemes had not taken the farmland much further out into the Wash and so it was an ideal spot from which to study and paint the wild fowl which frequent the area.

At this time also, one of Lincolnshire's famous poachers, Mr Mackenzie Thorpe, also known as Kenzie the 'Wild Goose Man', was a well known character in the district. Kenzie worked for Sir Peter, picking up some of his painting skills and producing his own interpretations of the local wild-life. His other adventures included clashes with the Royal gamekeeper at Sandringham and even a prison sentence for a dubious adventure. This interesting character attracted Prince Charles, who visited him at his council house and this led to the street being renamed Royal Close as a perpetual reminder.

All villages must change with the times or die and Sutton Bridge has shown itself well capable of changing with the times. It will still be a name to be reckoned with in the 21st century.

Swayfield 🐑

Swayfield is a small rural village of about 100 houses, some built of stone and some in brick, situated midway between the towns of Stamford, Grantham and Bourne.

Swayfield has the distinction of lying on the highest ground traversed by the railway between London and the Scottish border. During the age of the steam engine, the straight length of railway track through the village was used to test the engines for speed and it is here that the famous 'Mallard' engine broke the speed record for steam engines.

The church of St Nicholas is set 200 yards from the rest of the village, the reason being that the original village houses were all burned to the ground in the 17th century after an outbreak of plague, to rid the area of infection. Parts of the church date back to the 12th century and the original battlemented tower still stands complete with the three bells. The church was reconstructed in 1824. The chancel was left untouched but in 1875 the nave was rebuilt and made bigger, and windows provided for both the nave and the chancel. These were given in memory of a former rector, the Rev William Eagleton BA. The east window is a beautiful leaded window depicting the Nativity, Crucifixion and Resurrection. The font just inside the door is medieval.

Swayfield's other claim to fame is that it was here in 1588 that one of the beacons was lit in a chain across the country to warn of the threat of invasion by the Spaniards. (The reason the beacon was so far inland was that they were set along the Lincolnshire Edge). In 1988 Swayfield once again had a beacon to commemorate the quatercentenary of the Spanish Armada, this beacon can be seen at the end of Church Lane.

The village, though small is fairly self-contained, with its own shop, post office, village hall and public house, the Royal Oak, which are all found in the middle of the village. The oldest part of the pub, with its stone walls and oak beams, dates from the 17th century, as has been confirmed by historical records which state that Cromwell once stayed in 'the old inn at Swayfield'. The village also possessed its own primary school until 1982, when it was closed down and the twelve pupils transferred to nearby Corby Glen.

The village of Swayfield, situated as it is two miles from the A1 and less than an hour's drive from Lincoln, Nottingham, Leicester and Peterborough, has grown rapidly in the last ten years, as more people working in cities seek sanctuary in the countryside for their homes and families. However, there remains a feeling of friendliness and community spirit in the village which has lost none of its rural charm.

Swineshead 🐖

With a population of around 3,000, Swineshead is one of the larger parishes in the borough of Boston. It lies six miles west of Boston on the edge of the fens and the village extends for over two miles along what was the A17 to Sleaford until the village was bypassed in 1985. The village has a station on the Grantham to Boston railway.

Swineshead take its name from an inlet or channel called the Swin, which formerly ran up from the sea to the Market Place. The sea at one time being much nearer, the limit or head of the water was naturally called Swins Head – hence Swineshead.

A Cistercian abbey was founded here in the 12th century. It is said that King John sought shelter here in 1216 after losing his baggage and equipment in the Wash, before dying three days later at Newark. The abbey was closed in 1536 at the first Dissolution of the Monasteries. The site was granted to Edward Lord Clinton (later Earl of Lincoln).

Remains of a Danish encampment (a circular site called the Manwarings, pronounced 'Mannerings') is located north of Abbey Road. Roman relics have been unearthed nearby and there are traces of an early motte and bailey castle. It is thought salt pans were worked in what is known as Low grounds. Flint axe heads have also been found in the area.

Swineshead became a market town in the Middle Ages with a market held every Thursday. In the rather attractive market square the old stocks and butter cross are reminders of the village's status.

Cheese Hill takes its name from the cheese sold on the site when the market was in existence. Tarry Hill was so called because a very large family lived in the vicinity, the records refer to the baptism of the 27th child of William and Sarah Tarry.

There are several attractive period houses in the village, two former windmills and near the square the parish church of St Mary the Virgin, built in the 13th century. Although the chancel was rebuilt in 1847 the rest of the church is of the Decorated period, and the handsome tower is capped by a lantern and short spire which are local landmarks.

Swineshead has been designated a main village in the Lincolnshire structure plan. The market place was noted as a designated area of conservation, with consequent tightening of design standards.

Many of the shops in the High Street and Market Place have changed hands several times. The old public house in the High Street known as the Black Swan is now a private house named 'The Mucky Duck' (its nickname when it was a pub). The grocer's and general dealer's once owned by the Metcalf family is now a tea room and art gallery combined. It is known as the 'Jack O'Lantern' because of the jackdaws in the trees close by the lantern at the top of the church tower. New houses are springing up at the side of the old buildings in the High Street, and many other areas. The beautiful old school on Station Road is now a private house and workshop.

Swineshead has the charm of a village with many amenities of a town, including a minimarket, a grocer's and an electrician's, a chemist, a doctor's surgery, hairdressing and beauty salons, pubs, restaurants, a florist, a garage, a furniture shop, a wool shop and a post office.

There are two ponds in Swineshead, Mackays Pitt – renovated in a

Swineshead village

153

village project, and one in Coles Lane which was improved and stocked with wildfowl by people in the village. This is enjoyed by many villagers and visitors with children, who enjoy feeding the ducks and geese.

There are two Methodist churches in Swineshead, one in the farming area known as Fenhouses. This church was remodelled in the mid 1920s and later in the 1980s when the house which was attached was demolished. Swineshead Methodist church in the High Street, the 'new' part built about 1900, has been demolished. The older part is to be renovated and this part is a Grade II listed building.

Syston

Syston, four miles from Grantham, lies beside the lovely hillside park of Syston Hall, the park being the scene of inter-collegiate motor cycle races prior to the Second World War.

The beautiful church of St Mary is a partly rebuilt Norman church, with later additions.

The Old Hall in the village is the home of the Thorold family, the current baronet being in residence.

Until fairly recent times the village was owned by the Thorold family but most of the houses are now privately owned and new homes in the village have done nothing to destroy the peace and tranquillity.

Syston is the 'Willingham' of Sir Walter Scott's novel *The Heart of Midlothian.*

Tattershall with Thorpe

Tattershall is a busy village, situated between the rivers Bain and Witham. Robert Tateshale gave his name to the place when he built a stone castle, forerunner of the present brick keep of Tattershall Castle, built by his son, also Robert.

This Robert gave King John a trained goshawk in return for the privilege of holding a weekly market, of which the market cross is now the only remnant. Today, the market place is often filled with cars, whose owners go to shop at what is claimed to be the biggest village supermarket in the county.

Tattershall Fair, celebrated at the end of September, when there were amusements on the green and animals were brought from miles around

154

to be sold has died out, but the energetic friendly committee organise celebrations on that date, and donate the proceeds to local good causes.

The imposing brick keep of Tattershall Castle dominates the village and is a landmark for many miles over the surrounding fens. For those who are agile enough to climb the unusual spiral stone staircase up to the summit, on a clear day there is the reward of seeing a wonderful panorama, as far as Lincoln Cathdral and Boston Stump.

Lord Curzon of Kedleston saved the castle from dereliction when he bought it for the nation. The magnificent stone fireplaces were already crated to commence the journey to America. Now, the property belongs to the National Trust, including a museum and gift shop in the guard house.

Holy Trinity church, a vast edifice, is close by the castle. In 1989, the 550th anniversary of this building, successor of an earlier place of worship, was celebrated by the restored and replaced great east window. After other stained glass windows were taken to Burghley House and St Martin's Stamford, the only stained glass in Holy Trinity was in the east window, a jigsaw of colours.

Close by the church are the bedeshouses, now occupied by six people, but originally built for 13 poor of the parish in the 15th century. Benefits for these men and women were cauldrons of coal and lengths of red flannel for petticoats.

A large part of Tattershall around the market place is a conservation area, including houses/shops constructed from bricks which formed the courtyard wall of the castle, the house of Tom Thumb, whose burial slab is in the nave aisle of the church.

Several craftspeople have their homes and shops in Tattershall, providing a service for villagers and tourists.

Although this village has a rich past, it is preparing for the future. Lakes left from sand and gravel workings have been developed with surrounding land as a leisure centre, where caravan people spend holidays, fishing or at sport. Further expansion includes lakeside holiday homes, a heated swimming pool, sauna and other amenities.

During the summer, the only working beam engine in the country steams on the first Sunday of each month, by the side of the Witham.

Thorpe is a fast growing hamlet on the road from Tattershall to Woodhall Spa. Mentioned in the Domesday Book as Torp, it was then superior in status.

The Blue Bell Inn is an ancient hostelry on a drovers' road, and has a priest's hole, relic of the Civil War.

Nature lovers have a wide scope at Thorpe, as the Woodland Trust has recently acquired Carr Wood. There are sand martins and other migratory birds among the sand and gravel workings, where pre-historic remains have been found.

Tealby 🐾

Tealby is a pretty village of some 500 inhabitants, set on the edge of the Lincolnshire Wolds, about mid-way between Lincoln and Grimsby. The Viking Way, a long distance footpath, passes through the village, which provides a welcome refreshment stop for walkers.

With the advantages of high ground and running water, it is likely to have been a settlement from earliest times. The hill on which the church stands was probably the site of a Saxon fort and the name itself shows its Viking origin. Under the name Tavelsbi, the village is mentioned in the Domesday Book and described as having four mills. In 1807 a ploughman turned up an earthen pot containing over 5,000 silver pennies, in mint condition, dating from the reign of Henry II. Coins from the Tealby Hoard, as it is known, are now in many collections, including the British Museum and the Usher Art Gallery.

The sites of seven water mills can be identified along the stream and two mill houses stand today. The corn mill at Tealby Thorpe is in working order and open to the public from time to time. The name Papermill Lane, near the church, shows another use for which the water power was formerly used.

John Wesley records preaching at Tealby five times between 1747 and 1786. At that time the village population was larger (861 in 1851). He describes the inhabitants as 'plain serious country people, very different from the wild unbroken herd to whom I preached at Horncastle in the evening'.

The beauty of the village comes from the golden limestone of the old cottages, the profusion and colour of the cottage gardens and the meandering stream, the river Rase, which skirts the village and is crossed by picturesque fords and bridges at each end. There is a fine Norman church, All Saints, with some interesting memorials, and a rare thatched public house, the King's Head, dating from 1357. The surviving Methodist chapel was built in 1819.

Charles Tennyson, uncle of the poet, built a romantic Gothic castle, Bayons Manor, here between 1836 – 42. He also added the surname

D'Eyncourt, recalling a remote ancestor. Unfortunately the house fell into disrepair after the Second World War and was finally demolished in 1962. However the Tennyson D'Eyncourts have left their mark on the village. Charles founded the school, a handsome building in the Gothic style, in 1857. It was burned down in 1889 and rebuilt the following year. Later members of the family built the village hall, the Tennyson D'Eyncourt Memorial Hall, which was opened in 1930. No member of the family now lives in the village.

Tetney

The village of Tetney is situated in the north-eastern part of Lincolnshire about two miles inland from the river Humber and the North Sea. Five or six miles away are the lovely rolling Lincolnshire Wolds.

An urn containing Anglo-Saxon silver coins was unearthed in 1945 and that is considered evidence that Tetney existed as a dwelling place a thousand years ago.

It was for many years a farming community but that has changed over the years. Farming still goes on, but as the population has increased, most of its workforce travels to Grimsby, to the town itself, to the docks and further along to the many factories along the Humber Bank.

The village is served by several provision shops, newsagents, a post office, one public house and a separate off-licence, also a butcher's shop and a coal merchant. A fried fish shop opens daily. Several smaller firms have started in workshops, among them a motor repair shop and stone garden ornaments. A petrol filling station is in the centre of the village and two garden centres on the outskirts.

Not many of the old houses and buildings have survived, but the village green, the so-called 'Green Hill', is still with us, complete with chestnut tree.

The ancient and beautiful church of St Peter and St Paul stands on the southern boundary, well tended and thriving. The Methodist chapel, St John's, stands in the centre of the village.

Not far from the church are the 'Blow Wells', several deep reservoirs of artesian water. Around these is a nature reserve of animals, birds and flowers, a very secluded and beautiful place.

Two miles away, on the coast lies the hamlet of Tetney Lock, through which flows the Navigation canal to the sea. At Tetney Lock is the RSPB bird sanctuary for many rare seabirds.

Along the Tetney Lock road are the enormous oil tanks served by the oil terminal on the coast. Oil is pumped through the 'Tank Farm' to the refineries inland.

The village has a fine modern primary school, where about 150 scholars are taught in comfortable surroundings. They have a good playground surrounded by a tree-planted area. This school replaced the old day school built by Methodists in 1856. The old school building is now a residential home for the elderly.

Also, comparatively new to the village is a large residential and nursing home.

The population of Tetney is about 1,600. Although this is an increase over the years, Tetney is still, by modern standards, a smallish village. By common consent, it will, for the foreseeable future, remain so. No large-scale development is planned or desired.

Theddlethorpe 🦋

Theddlethorpe is a marsh coastal village with two parishes, St Helen's and All Saints. There are two churches and a Methodist chapel and two public houses, one thatched, The King's Head, and the Penny Farthing. The small farms are mainly arable.

To the east of Theddlethorpe lies the sea and the dunes which form part of the Saltfleetby Nature Reserve, owned and administered partly by the Nature Conservancy Council and partly by the Lincolnshire and South Humberside Trust for nature conservation. The shoreline and dunes have been fashioned by seven centuries of wind and tide, depositing sand, flotsam and jetsam and building up sandbanks which are quickly colonised by maritime grasses and plants and then later by the invasive and prickly sea buckthorn, which provide food for visiting migratory and resident birds alike.

At times the sand dunes are swiftly chopped away by the winter storms to leave a sheer 'cliff face' of sand; although for the most part in recent years there has been much more build up of sand bank than encroachment by the sea at Theddlethorpe. On the older more established dunes, trees and bushes abound. As well as buckthorn there is hawthorn, wild rose, wild privet, elder and even a few fruit trees and bushes unwittingly brought as seed by birds.

With its varied habitat the reserve is home to a wide variety of insects, butterflies, birds and animals including foxes, rabbits, badgers and the rare natterjack toad. To maintain this habitat the dunes are carefully managed to prevent the more invasive species of bush and plant crowding out the less aggressive ones. This is achieved by carefully controlled cutting and grazing by cattle and sheep, resulting in areas of short turf where wild flowers can bloom and butterflies breed.

Life was hard on the marshes many years ago but the sandhills bordering the coast were wide and their dunes ideal for secretive hiding places. There were many stories of smugglers on the coast. Farm waggons and horses were used. They too would go out to sea to take the goods, gin and tobacco sometimes, hide them at the farms, then take them further inland. But the Preventive Officers were alert and penalties were very harsh.

Many years later came the lifeboat. Mr Bell from North End Farm was a crewman and signalman, and the farmhorses (one called *Beaut*) would take the boat out to sea, the men astride the horses. Today the field in which some of those horses grazed is part of the land belonging to the Gas Terminal.

Theddlethorpe became a national landmark in July 1972 when, after two years of construction work the North Sea Gas Terminal started its flow of gas into the national grid. The then Gas Council, now known as British Gas, bought the land. Some of this is leased to the American based company Conoco, the original finder and developer of the 'Viking Field' (this is the name of one of many gas fields in the North Sea). Most people refer to the terminal as Conoco, but in fact there are two different companies in operation – Conoco who 'bring the gas ashore' and British Gas who process it for industrial and domestic use and push it through to the national grid.

Theddlethorpe was apparently chosen for its strategic position between the two existing terminals of Easington near Hull and Bacton in Norfolk. At the time of the purchase of the land, the villagers were naturally worried about how the terminal would affect their lives and their landscape. But the terminal was built to strict design codes to make it as unobtrusive as possible and tree belts have been planted for a visual screen. After the initial worry of the villagers, the Gas Terminal has become part of the village with, on the whole very good relations between them and the local council and villagers. Although the terminal has not brought a great deal of local employment, it has benefited quite a few local businesses and made quite a large contribution to local amenities. A play area for children on the village playing field being one example.

A famous visitor to Theddlethorpe was the writer D. H. Lawrence. The shore's prospect pleased him and it fascinated him to walk on the wide shore; on one side the noisy restless waves ever changing and on the other side the silent, serene and sheltered sandhills.

St Helen's church, half hidden by trees at the side of the road, is not only used as a church but also as a community centre. Even so it is still a quiet retreat. It was almost entirely rebuilt in 1866 and its greatest treasure is the reredos of Caen stone dating back to 1400. The stone crucifix which once surmounted this reredos now stands in the recess. Just along the road from St Helen's church is the Methodist chapel, which retains its tiered pews. Its schoolroom is host to the monthly meetings of the Women's Institute and the Parish Council and is the visiting doctor's consulting room.

Last but not least is the now redundant church of All Saints. With its many treasures it is handsome enough to have earned the name of 'Cathedral of the Marsh'.

Thorpe-on-the-Hill

This small village is situated a few miles to the south-west of Lincoln. Thorpe-on-the-Hill is described in the North Kesteven District Council's draft village discussion document as being one of numerous 'Minor Villages'. Since that document was produced in November 1979 the population has risen from 372 to about 700.

The village contains a newly built primary school, which functions also as a village hall. It also has a post office with a small store, one public house, two churches and a motor engineer. Leisure activities include a bowls club, tennis courts, badminton, a Women's Institute and a youth club.

There is a regular bus service between Lincoln, which is approximately seven miles away and Newark, and the village is well served by mobile facilities which include a library, butcher and fishmonger.

Thurlby 🍂

Thurlby was a fairly small village until after the Second World War, agriculture being the main source of work, with very few people working outside the village. Everyone knew each other really well, quite a few were related. Then new houses began to spring up all around the village and most of the old cottages gradually disappeared. Now only four of the picturesque thatched cottages still remain.

The village, as its name suggests, has Danish connections, and the beautiful and ancient church, although mainly Norman and Early English, shows earlier work in that the lower parts of the tower are Saxon and there is a Saxon arch, lined with a later Norman arch, evidently for strength, giving access to the bell tower. As the church stands on the bank of the Roman Car Dyke, a canal or catchwater drain which runs between Lincoln and Peterborough, it is possible that the church may have replaced a Roman shrine.

The church is dedicated to St Firmin, one of only two with this dedication in England and is well worth a visit. There is also a Methodist church, and the two work well together for the welfare of the village, especially in youth work.

Thurlby and its hamlet of Northorpe are now joined by new building, and there are two settlements to the south, Obthorpe and Kates Bridge, both of ancient origin.

A Darby and Joan Club caters for the over 60s and is about 40 years old. Almond Court was built to house elderly people under the care of a warden and this means that there is quite a large percentage of retired people in the village.

A few years ago a very old woodland was lent and then sold to the Lincolnshire Nature Conservancy Trust and has been carefully looked after. It is known as Dole Wood and contains very old trees and plants and is open to the public occasionally. It is reached from Obthorpe Lane. More recently the same Trust has acquired the water meadows, known as slipes, on the banks of the river Glen which flows along the eastern boundary of the village between Thurlby and Baston Fens. A lot of tidying up work has been done there and visitors are very welcome.

A few years ago two ladies, members of the Lawrance family, who own land in the village, gave a field to be used as a playing field. This land has been developed, and as well as a playing field there is a modern village hall and a new primary school, connected to the hall and used by school and village on a 'Chance to Share' basis. A Cup was also given by the two ladies to be presented annually to the person or group of persons who have done outstanding voluntary work for the benefit of the village.

And last, but not least, there is a ghost, Nanny Rutt, who haunts a pool in Elsea Wood (to the north of the village) named Nanny Rutt's Well after her. She was supposed to have been murdered by her boyfriend, and her body thrown into the pool!

Uffington ✿

If the WI had been in existence in Victorian times, Uffington's Lady Charlotte Bertie would doubtless have been a driving force.

Not only did the magnificent Charlotte bear ten children in 13 years, but when her ironmaster husband Joshua Guest died, she had no hesitation in taking over the ironworks herself. She spoke Italian and French, read Latin and Greek, and still found time to add medieval Welsh, Hebrew and Persian to her repertoire. And almost to the the end of her life, she is said to have worked every day at knitting red woollen comforters for London cabbies.

Charlotte's ancestors, the Berties, came to Uffington in the 1670s having bought their estate from the dissolute second Duke of Buckingham. Their name lives on in the village's popular Bertie Arms Inn, parts of which are said to go back 300 years.

The family built an imposing mansion, Uffington House, held to be one of the great homes of Lincolnshire. Destroyed by a tragic fire in 1904, its delicate 19th century orangery stood majestically alone until only a few years ago (1980) when it was demolished and the stone used to rebuild boundary walls on the estate.

Uffington's other pub, the Gainsborough Lady, was owned by the Trollope family until the 1970s and was formerly known as the Trollope Arms, a name which then caused little excitement. It blazed into local publicity again in 1986, when developers of new homes in the village rejected a suggestion to call the site Trollope Close. They feared its closeness to the word 'trollop', meaning a loose woman, might make it difficult to sell the houses. In the end the district council stepped in and backed up parish councillors who wanted to honour a family whose branches had produced the great English novelist Anthony Trollope.

It was Charlotte Bertie's ancestors who gave the parish church of St Michael and All Angels its distinctive wrought iron gates at the entrance to the churchyard in the 17th century. Each February visitors to the church walk between them into a pristine white carpet of hundreds of snowdrops, and in the field alongside stand Uffington's Five Sentinels, a group of tall and protective trees which create a distinctive silhouette against the mellow stone of increasingly sought-after country cottages.

Uffington has become a popular haven for commuters, who travel to work each day in the towns of Stamford, Spalding and Bourne, and the city of Peterborough. There is a community post office but no shops, but a village school provides bustle several times a day and sends play-time laughter drifting across the Sentinels' field. Last century Uffington had a canal and its own railway station and a poor house – the name 'Poor End' lingered on in that part of the village for years.

Other vanished street names include the picturesque Witwath, or White Ford, and the road to the neighbouring village of Essendine used to be described in rather gruesome terms as 'the road to Hangman's Corner'.

In this rural setting on the edge of the fen country, you might think yourself a million miles away from senseless vandalism. But Uffington's churchgoers still remember the February Sunday in 1988 when they arrived for morning service to find windows smashed, prayerbooks strewn around the church, gravestones vandalised and a valuable 17th century chandelier badly damaged. Two young men – neither of them local – were later convicted of criminal damage. Generously, the rector prayed for them, though he was to tell the local press that had he caught the pair in the act, prayer might not have been his first reaction!

A small community which enjoys making its own recreation, Uffington has a village hall which plays host twice a week to practices by Stamford Town Band. And despite the intrusion of the modern world, it is still possible to get away from workday pressures by one of the most pleasant of rural relaxations – walking along the meadows, lanes and river banks where blossom hangs lush in summer, berries still abound in autumn, and where wild birds and animals reveal nature's richness at every season of the changing years.

Upton & Kexby 🌿

Upton is a village of ancient origin, four miles south-east of Gainsborough and 13 miles north of Lincoln. To the south is the neighbouring village of Kexby, with a population and size similar to that of Upton. Together the two villages, with a total population of some 700 people, form the ecclesiastical parish of Upton-cum-Kexby.

The parish church which stands impressively on slightly higher ground in the centre of Upton village, is dedicated to All Saints and serves both villages. The original church which stood on these foundations was an early Norman structure consisting of nave and chancel only. About the middle of the 13th century the church was considerably rebuilt and a northern aisle and western tower added and the chancel lengthened. In 1767 the tower fell down and a new one with a circular west window was built. Considerable and much needed restoration took place between 1873 and 1876 under the direction of James Fowler, of Louth.

The tower contains six bells, the oldest dating to 1641. In the vestry is a large painted board, detailing the gift of two acres of land left to the poor of Upton in 1697.

The village inn, the Rose and Crown, with its large car park, faces the parish church across the High Street. The inn, which has recently been tastefully refurbished, was built in 1953, replacing one of ancient origin.

In both villages, new housing development blends well with the older mellow brick and tiled houses and farms. A number of Victorian buildings, including the old school, built with an attractive locally produced brick, give an interesting contrast and are a visible reminder of the thriving brick making business that once existed in Kexby.

A number of old farmhouses and barns, together with some dwellings listed as of architectural interest can be seen, the oldest being the Hall at Upton, with its high walled garden and small plantation. Local tradition links the Hall with Parliamentary troops during the Civil War.

Upton has a small, but charming, well kept Methodist chapel built in 1822, with a schoolroom of mellow brick added 30 years later. Among the memorials inside are two large brass plaques listing the names of the fallen, together with the names of those who served from Upton and Kexby in the two World Wars. The chapel is one of the oldest in the county still in regular use. The two chapels that once served the village of Kexby are now closed, but the buildings remain, converted to other uses.

Both villages have extensive field paths, all well signposted and maintained, leading to Heapham, Willingham, Knaith and Gainsborough, with magnificent views of the villages, the Trent valley and the Lincolnshire Cliff. The paths cross interesting and varied fields, including some meadows where the pre-enclosure method of strip farming can still be easily traced.

In the centre of Kexby, facing the green, is the village well which supplied the village with drinking water before the installation of a piped supply. Now preserved, the well, which is spring fed, was never known to run dry and in times of drought supplied water over a wide area. The spring may at one time have fed a small tributary of the river Till, which flows through low farmland to the east of both villages. Some historians are of the opinion that the Danes, who first inhabited Kexby, were able to navigate their boats along the Till to a mooring pool near the settlement. The river, now little more than a stream, is home for a variety of wildlife, including the kingfisher.

A new village hall has recently been opened and offers a variety of sporting and social activities.

Both villages offer a wide selection of services, including a well stocked general store and post office, a fish and chip shop and a blacksmith's shop where the ring of the smith's hammer on the anvil can be heard. To the north of Upton is the old Royal Air Force Sturgate airfield, now used by Eastern Airways.

Utterby 🐚

The village of Utterby, population 277 at the 1981 census, lies on the main A16 trunk road, four miles north of Louth.

Utterby is not recorded in the Domesday Book but almost certainly existed in earlier times, the name derived from the Danish 'Utter's Bye' meaning a habitation belonging to Utter. It may well have existed even earlier, particularly with the proximity of the pre-Roman road from Louth to the ford at Barton on Humber.

The manor of Utterby was granted to Henry-de-Elye in 1220, and the name of Elye has been associated with the village for many centuries. The present manor house in Church Lane was built in 1639, and bears the coat of arms of the Elye family. This fine house was altered and enlarged in Victorian times. White's Directory of 1856 tells us that Reverend Thomas Eley was at that time the lord of the manor and patron of St Andrew's church.

The present St Andrew's church probably originated in the 14th century, though the list of rectors displayed in the church goes back to 1220. This charming small church contains some interesting memorials, particularly the effigy of the 14th century rector William de Cumberworth, and a hatchment of William Davison dated 1702. The south porch has some fascinating carvings around the doorway arch.

Beyond the church is a 14th century packhorse bridge, thought to be one of only three in the country. This crosses a small stream, and was used in olden times by drovers bringing their animals from summer grazing on the marsh to market. A house nearby is still known as Drovers' Yard, where the drover and his animals could stay overnight. This bridge may also have been part of the salt route – packhorses carrying the salt from the coast to the inland towns.

There are two other houses of note in Church Lane. Utterby House is Georgian and was built about 1800, and The Old Rectory, designed by James Fowler, in 1863. There has been more building in recent years, but with a protection order on the many fine trees in the lane its attractive leafy appearance has been maintained. The south side of the lane is within the Wolds Area of Outstanding Natural Beauty, and every effort is made to maintain this standard.

Utterby is primarily a farming community. The eastern lanes all lead to farms and are not through-roads. Holywell Lane, as its name implies, passes a holy well, which in ancient times was considerd to have medicinal properties. Pilgrims who visited the well left their bandages on the surrounding bushes.

Chapel Lane contains the Wesleyan Methodist chapel, dated 1854, where services are held each Sunday. Utterby had three chapels at one time, the Primitive and Free Methodist chapels being no longer in use. Also in Chapel Lane is the recently built Benson Court, a group of homes for the elderly called after Mrs Katherine Benson who owned the manor in the last century. She was an eccentric lady, who fought to prevent the railway coming near to the village. The line did run about a mile east of Utterby where there was a halt, but alas, it fell to the Beeching axe. Mrs Benson was also responsible for the building of The Round House in Grange Lane, though it is octagonal in shape.

There are many fine gardens in Utterby, perhaps the most notable

Packhorse bridge and St Andrew's Church, Utterby

being at Midlane House, in Grange Lane. The house was originally two farm cottages, but the present brickwork dates from about 1780. Beside Grange Lane is the village green, occasionally used for local events; and on the other side of the green is the Parish Room where various organisations meet.

Utterby has just one shop, but an excellent one which caters well for the needs of the village, and supplies full post office services. There is also a regular bus service to Grimsby and Louth – something quite rare in this rural county. Utterby still has a thriving primary school though the older chidren have to travel to Louth.

Waddington 🪶

The Viking Way, which runs through Waddington, is a reminder that the Celts, farming the cliff top west of the Roman Ermine Street some 1,500 years ago, were overwhelmed by those warriors from the sea.

The Domesday Book reveals Waddington's development as an agricultural community. Signs of its medieval five fields system still show in furlong ridges by Milking Hill, later called 'Somerslay's Lane'. The farmers' homesteads were established in the well-drained, cliff-edge village itself, leaving the legacy of numerous fine houses and barns. Thanks to the vigilance of the Parish Council and the Residents Association, these buildings now enhance a delightful conservation area.

The High Street and the Hilltop, running parallel from north to south, form the framework for the eleven linking lanes, which are at the heart of this well-wooded 'ladder' village. The majority of the houses date from the 16th century onwards in the local limestone. Their roofs are bright with red pantiles, originally moulded from the clays of the vale below. Some stonewalled lanes still carry the names of early farmers, Timms and Capps, whilst Bartoft House reminds us of a prominent 13th century Norman knight.

The present population of 5,000 is almost equally divided between the old village on the cliff and the modern growth of estates, which have developed downhill to the west. The hill itself is a constant barrier to a desirable unity in village life. The population of the Western Lowfields tends to be Lincoln orientated.

To the east, lies the major RAF station of Waddington, opened in 1917 as a training centre for the Royal Flying Corps, and now being

Blind Lane, Waddington

brought back to full strength to operate within the NATO Airborne Early Warning System. Since the extensive runway lies north to south, other villages bear a greater brunt of the noise overhead.

The presence of the station, which in 1959 received the Freedom of the City of Lincoln, is a great asset to village life. Not only is it generous with help and facilities, but the presence of its personnel makes feasible many activities and amenities within the village itself. Swimming and Drama Clubs, Adult Education classes, together with the Scouts, Guides, Cubs and Brownies, appreciate the use of camp facilities and the WRVS is indebted to it for the cooking for the meals-on-wheels service. The outstandingly frequent bus service is thanks to their indirect influence. In 1987, a memorial clock was presented to the village and erected in the shopping precinct, on the occasion of the station and the village together playing host to the Australian and British members of the 463 and 467 Squadrons, who had served here during the Second World War. Many villagers are ex-RAF personnel.

The impressive village hall stands in 21 acres of playing field uphill, whilst a well-designed community centre and field serve the lower village. There are two County primary schools.

A traditional easy relationship exists between the Methodist church in the High Street, the Roman Catholic church on the camp and the parish church of St Michael and All Angels, which stands on a commanding site in the centre of the old village. The fine peal of bells remains as a reminder of the night of the 8th May 1941, when a land mine was dropped by enemy aircraft on the empty Saxon church. Only eleven years later, a spacious, light and modern church was dedicated on the site, to continue to act as a focus to life in Waddington.

Shopping precincts, post offices and corner shops offer a wide shopping range. There is a doctor's surgery uphill but no chemist. A branch of the county library opens thrice weekly. Nearby, in 1840, lived George Boole, the famous mathematician, who was awarded the Royal Society's Gold Medal for Mathematical Analysis.

Of three public houses, the Wheatsheaf still reflects the continued agricultural background of this dormitory village. The old race course, which became the site for the camp, gave names to the Horse and Jockey and the Three Horse Shoes. The two former inns supply meals, along with a long-established fish and chip shop and a new Chinese take-away. There are a number of small industries in the village. An engineering firm has developed from the family business of the village blacksmith, who shod the racehorses in the last century.

A windmill stands, in some disrepair, on the southern cliff edge, a successor to a postmill that previously enhanced the northern boundary, near the site of a Roman kiln. A fire station, manned by eleven part-timers, stands near the main crossroads on the busy Lincoln-Grantham road.

Welton 🐾

The name of Welton by Lincoln distinguishes this parish from seven other Weltons in England.

It is a charming village with a lot of the old houses built from locally made bricks of attractive colourings and Lincolnshire stone.

The Black Bull Inn and the church are centred around the village green. The old blacksmith's is now garages. The beck rises from Oldman head spring and meanders through the village and is now the home of many mallard ducks. The original village pump still holds pride of place.

The first church was built in the 11th century and a second built in 1250, but it was then destroyed by fire in 1442. It was fully rebuilt in 1823. On Sunday 29th August 1847 it was struck by lightning, when one person was killed and many injured.

The church of St Mary which we know today has had extensions and improvements over the years. A giant boulder from the Ice Age stands by the porch. In the church are two stained glass windows on the north side, one to the memory of Dr Richard Smith who founded the Blue Coat school in Lincoln. The other is to the memory of those who died in the First and Second World Wars from RAF Scampton. It was dedicated by Canon Hunt, a former vicar and padre at Scampton in 1918. Nearby is the Methodist church and combined services are often held.

Six prebends were given to Welton by Oliver Cromwell and some of the roads in Welton have been named after them – Brinkhall, Beckhall, Rivehall, Westhall and Painshall. The old school was built in 1826 and has now been sold and converted into two dwellings and a wool shop.

Saxon House, a community home, is so named as it is built on an old Saxon burial ground – remains were found in 1971 when foundations were being dug and they were later interred in the churchyard.

The William Farr comprehensive school is named after a former vicar who bought RAF huts after the Second World War to secure a secondary school for the village. St Mary's primary school is situated to the rear of the health centre, clinic and library.

Cottage at Welton

Welton is an expanding village with many private houses built on estates in recent years. Stonecliffe Park is well laid out with residential mobile homes and its own social club. There are council owned flats at Cliffe Park and Park House for senior citizens, as well as a few bungalows and a small number of council houses.

Many of the shops have been converted from old buildings and part of the butcher's shop near the church is 14th century. The old cobbler's shop next door is now used by the church for donated items to sell for charities. The stocks once stood on the pinfold but all that is left now is a small piece of land in front of the pet food shop. A modern Co-op shop was built a few years ago and now incorporates the post office. The paper shop and Memory Lane Antiques share the building that was the post office and general stores for many years.

Many social activities take place at the village hall, built in 1962. To the rear is the bowling club, well attended by residents. A thriving Sports and Social Club is situated in the playing field where members may play darts and pool as well as outdoor activities such as football and cricket, and there is also a children's playground.

Welton le Marsh

Welton le Marsh is a pretty little village situated about seven miles from Skegness and five miles from Alford.

The main reservoir for the Anglian Water Board supplying Skegness and the coastal strip with water is situated at the west of the village.

At one time a Roman road crossed part of the village but its name, which means 'land enclosed by trees', was first given to a Saxon settlement. The village is indeed very proud of its wood, extending to approximately one square mile. Until recently the oak stakes and posts from Welton wood were sought by farmers from a very wide area. In the middle of the wood is a large privately owned house known as Thwaite Hall. This stands on the site of an old castle and was at one time a monastic cell used by the monks of Thorton Abbey.

At the north-east end of the village is a mound known as Castle Hill which is thought to date back to the Iron Age.

The Methodist chapel, still in use, was built in 1875 and is approached by a winding, ascending path. The parish church, dedicated to St Martin, was originally built of local white stone, but on 9th April 1791 the tower fell down, demolishing most of the church. Rebuilding commenced and a new church was opened in October 1792. In 1914 the original 14th century font was found in a field near the church being used as a cattle trough. This was restored and is much prized by the villagers.

There is a magnificent panoramic view from the road leading westward towards the Louth road. On clear days it is possible to see as far as Mablethorpe to the north and Boston to the south, and even the cliffs of Hunstanton are visible.

West Ashby ✺

West Ashby is a village two miles north of Horncastle on the A153. It includes the hamlets of Midthorpe, Farthorpe and Furzehills (which was once known as Northorpe, a plague village).

It appears as 'Aschebi' in the Domesday Book of 1086, when it belonged to William the Conqueror. The Bishops of Carlisle were lords of the manor and patrons of the benefice from 1229.

All Saints' church is one of the largest churches in the area, said to date back originally to the 13th century. The present building is thought to have been built in the reign of Henry VII between the years 1485 and 1509. The tower was extensively restored in 1871, as a memorial to the Victorian ballad writer Charlotte Alington Barnard, who composed under the pen name of 'Claribel'. It contains three bells (not in use) and eight tubular bells. In 1903 a clock was placed in the tower by Mr Basset in memory of his mother.

Around the walls of the church there are a number of memorial tablets to members of prominent local families. Perhaps the most interesting of these is the tablet on the north wall of the chancel, in memory of one Richard Calthrop. Calthrop was a midshipman in the Royal Navy and fell at the battle of Algiers in 1816. The tablet gives, in unusual and dramatic detail, the story of the young hero's death, and is a vivid evocation of a naval action of those times.

The public elementary school was erected on the corner of the Main Road and Manor Lane in 1874 by public subscription, at a cost of £300, for 100 children. It closed its doors for the last time on 31st December 1980, and has now been sympathetically converted into a house, with little structural alteration.

Notable buildings in the village include the manor house built in 1840. The Grove, once the home of the Elmhirst family, is said to be home to several ghosts. West Ashby House is a Queen Anne mansion, formerly used by the Bishops of Carlisle. The front door and portico are said to have come from Captain Cook's house in London.

By the middle of the 19th century the village was self sufficient, with everything from a baker to a wheelwright. Today the only facilities are a pub and restaurant. This is reflected in the population, which was 584 in 1841 compared with 224 today.

Sand and gravel are excavated near the river Bain, and windsurfing takes place on one of the disused pits. In 1977 archaeologists found a Bronze Age burial ground near the gravel pits at Furzehills.

A Country Club is being erected down Shearmans Wath, with a golf range and facilities for snooker and coarse fishing.

West Keal & Keal Cotes 🐟

This village and hamlet are about three and a half miles from Spilsby.

The village of West Keal has not been over-developed by new buildings. The upper part is known as High Barns and many years ago the villagers lived in the area around the church. Exciting archaeological discoveries of flint weapons, spears and arrow heads have been made.

This is a busy farming region, mainly corn, potatoes and sugar beet. The eastern farm is mainly sheep and people travelling through often enjoy seeing the lambs at play. In the last few years oilseed rape has been widely grown and its bright yellow flowers can be seen for miles.

There is a cafe on the main road, but no shop or post office now. Many years ago there was a beer shop. The blacksmith's building is still there but now silent.

The village hall and grounds were originally a Church of England school. This is a great asset to village life and is used by many organisations including the WI. The views and walks in the locality are enjoyed by many; the Boston Ramblers come every year and afterwards have a barbecue in the village hall grounds.

St Helen's church is built upon a southernmost ridge of the Wolds, standing between the Wolds and fenland. The steps in the porch are said to be in line with the top of Boston Stump (St Botolph's church). The view is magnificent, on a clear day one can see the sea. There is little doubt that an earlier church stood here (this one is mainly late 12th to early 13th century) for an entry in the Domesday Book records of West Keal, or West Rekale as it was then called, 'There is a church there, and

West Keal and Keal Cotes were once part of a large country estate with a squire. A few properties and some land still belong to the estate, including the village hall.

Keal Cotes had an elementary Church of England school for many years. It was built in 1854 by Col R. Amcotts of Hackthorn to hold 85 girls and boys. The hamlet also had a Wesleyan chapel with Sunday school, built in 1891. Both eventually closed, and after closure were used intermittently to hold Church of England services. These were popular with many of the older people, who preferred to attend services near their homes. The former school, refurbished, is now a flourishing parish hall.

Whaplode ❧

Whaplode is a village situated five miles from Holbeach and eight miles from Spalding. It has changed a great deal over the last few decades.

The road by the post office once led to the end of the road and onto the highway, where there was a mill that ground the corn into flour and cattle feed. It had been there since Whaplode itself began. There were ten mills of this kind round Whaplode, as the fields held nothing but grain, potatoes, and of course grass. Quite close to the mill there was a baker's and the smell of new bread filled the air.

One old house in the village was once the harbourmaster's house, and people from the fens – 'Whaplode, St Catherine and Sutton St James' – had to pay a toll at the gate before they could get into Holbeach, as there used to be a waterway to the main road from the village. The monks from Crowland (or Croyland) came up the river by coracle from Stamford to build St Mary's church at Whaplode.

It is an 11th century church, so very grand but simple in its interior. Inside there is the 17th century Irby Tomb, where an effigy of Sir Anthony Irby and his wife lie with their children kneeling beside them. There is also a Methodist chapel in Whaplode and it was almost always full. There were farms around it and the voices of the farm labourers and their wives rang out on Sunday in competition with the church! There was a toffee shop and a fish and chip shop in the village.

But all that was many years ago and Whaplode has completely changed its face. The Bell and Bowl pub and its surrounding cottages have been flattened and the land bought by D. A. Green, Construction

Engineers. All that is left on that side of the road is the village hall, which had been the old schoolhouse.

The post office still stands but has a bungalow next to it. There are houses where there used to be fields and bungalows and houses where the old mill stood. The bakery is a house, the toffee shop is a large shop and garage. There are now three garages, a fish shop, five builders, four electricians and two lorry hauliers.

The station house is private and the train lines have been taken up so that there is only the memory of the trains that used to go through. The almshouses are still there, but the large old vicarage has been sold and a new vicarage built. The churchyard has given up its gravestones and is green grass with a few flower beds.

Wickenby ♣

Wickenby, known as Wichingbee in the Domesday Book, lies approximately eleven miles north-east of Lincoln and has a present day population of 177, which is likely to increase due to recent building. This village includes the hamlet of Westlaby.

Apart from the church the village has no centre, but is scattered along the approach roads with large tracks of farmland in between and the beck running along one side.

The old manor house, now four dwellings, thought to have been built in the 15th/16th century, is a listed building. Part of the old moat can be seen across the fields, while on the Chapel Field opposite the results of ridge and furrow farming are still evident.

In Wickenby wood, mentioned in the Domesday Book, the habitat for numerous wild flowers has been preserved. The railway station, now disused, lies near the wood about half a mile from the centre of the village. The old coal and cattle yards remain and the house is now a private residence.

The ancient stone church of St Peter and St Lawrence is in the late Perpendicular style and was restored in 1878, when the tower was added. The Methodist chapel, built in the same year, was converted in 1972 into a remarkable little theatre, privately owned. It is known as the Broadbent Theatre. Here professional travelling companies present excellent modern theatre, while amateurs also produce plays of a high standard.

The village school, originally built in 1842 and rebuilt in 1879, was used until quite recently and is now a private house.

Wickenby airfield, built for and used in the Second World War by the Lancaster bombers, lies on the first rise above the Lincoln shelf. From it there is an excellent view of Lincoln Cathedral, especially ethereal when floodlit. The airfield is still used by a private flying club. On it there is an impressive memorial to the 1,080 men of No 1 Group Bomber Command, 12 and 626 Squadrons RAF Wickenby, who failed to return from their missions. It takes the form of Icarus with burnt wings falling from the sky and is made out of twisted bomber metal.

There is a flourishing haulage and coal business in the centre of the village. This, together with other smaller enterprises and airfield developments, provides employment for a number of residents.

The village continues to grow and recently the building of a number of prestigious houses and bungalows has resulted in an increasing commuting population in an otherwise rural community.

Willingham by Stow

Willingham by Stow, mentioned in the Domesday Book, lies on the B1241 road some six miles south of Gainsborough and twelve miles north of Lincoln.

It has always been a mainly arable farming community, with 20 farmers working the land in the late 19th century. The same acreage today, however, is cultivated by just seven farmers.

The attractive St Helen's church, dating from the 11th and 14th centuries, has registers dating back to 1562. The nave and chancel were rebuilt in 1880 by Mrs Caroline Reynard in memory of her husband, who was rector here from 1875 to 1878. The tower houses six bells, three of which were recast in 1905, at which time three new ones were added. The cost of this was borne by Mr R. C. Bacon of Willingham House. The large stained glass east window is a memorial to the Hawke family. The Rev Edward Lord Hawke was rector from 1853 to 1874. His son was perhaps better known as he went on to play cricket for the Yorkshire County Club and for the MCC. St Helen's is now one of a group of parish churches cared for by the rector at Stow.

In the High Street lies the Methodist chapel built in 1885 and the County primary school built in 1818. There are school registers going back to 5th February 1877.

Although several shops flourished in the village at one time, there is now only a post office cum general store and a farm shop. Two public houses are still thriving – the Half Moon in the High Street and the Fox and Hounds in Gainsborough Road, while a modern doctor's surgery and dispensary are to be found at the bottom of the village.

Several of the older properties have been modernised in recent years, while infilling with new houses has been selectively allowed by the planning authorities. Willingham has not however been spoiled as yet by any large-scale housing development. Quite a few families have lived in the village for over 50 years – and indeed some for over a century, but increasingly this area is attracting workers who commute to either Lincoln or Gainsborough, and older people who have chosen to spend their retirement years here. A friendly atmosphere helps Willingham organisations to flourish, the village hall being the focal point of the various recreational groups.

Walking round the outskirts of the village one crosses and recrosses the river Till, which has been widened in recent years to prevent flooding. A tree-planting scheme was undertaken in 1978, financed by local inhabitants with local authority support. Willing volunteers planted the many trees which now enhance the approaches to the village, and these complement the longer established trees which give Willingham a most attractive setting.

Witham on the Hill 🐑

Witham on the Hill, once known as Witham-Super-Montem, is a small village with a population of less than 200. The parish church of St Andrew stands in the centre, and, as the village is on high ground, the spire is visible from a considerable distance.

The church is a Norman stone building, and possesses examples of many styles of later architecture. The Norman font has an elaborate canopy, behind which is a small lancet window, the oldest in the church. Witham church has possessed a clock for over 400 years; this is one of the earliest instances known of a clock in a church tower dating back to before the invention of the pendulum.

The strange position of the tower, standing at the south and away from the nave, is a remarkable feature and differentiates this church from all its neighbours. The tower was rebuilt in 1738, after it had collapsed. The story is told in White's 1856 Directory of Lincolnshire :

'The spire with a great part of the tower fell down in 1738, whilst the ringers, having rung some merry peals, were regaling themselves in a neighbouring inn. The steeple was rebuilt in a plainer but more substantial manner'.

According to White, Witham's misfortunes continued in 1773, when the inn, the vicarage, the tithe barn and other buildings burned down.

The Victorian school room, built close to the church in 1847, which is now the church hall, is inscribed with the motto: 'Train up a child in the way he should go and when he is old he will not part from it'.

Robert Harrington, one of Bourne's greatest benefactors, was born in Witham. The Harrington vault is under the high altar, and a mural brass commemorates Sir Richard Harrington and his wife, Robert's grandparents, who died in 1558 and 1565 respectively. The estate then passed to the Johnson family.

Witham Hall, a fine stone mansion in Queen Anne style, set in 15 acres of landscaped gardens, was built in 1752, by Rev Woolsey Johnson. Rev Woolsey Johnson was also responsible for the enclosure of open fields in the parish – a major event at that time.

In 1903 Walter Fenwick bought the house, and 'Squire' Fenwick was responsible for moving the village pub. The Black Dog, opposite the gates of the Hall at the turn of the century, had new stables built. The Squire got tired of losing his grooms to the Black Dog and had the Six Bells built at the other end of the village. Up until then housing was grouped around the Hall and along Bottom Street, but with the move of the pub, all new housing was built along the road, towards the pub, and away from the old centre of the village.

Palace Farm was once the manor house, with villager's huts and later houses clustered around it. It dates back to the 11th century, and is situated close to the church. The name is derived from its having been the former southern palace of the Bishops of Lincoln, being conveniently situated only a day's ride from Lincoln. King John is said to have stayed at Palace Farm, shortly before his death at Newark, on the 19th of October 1216. The remaining home is one third of the original, which was destroyed by fire.

In a neighbouring field is a 17th century dovecote. Doves were then kept as a food source, to be eaten either fresh or salted in the winter. Close to the church are the old stocks in a good state of preservation. However, the stocks were covered over in very recent times. The top bar was used in bonfire celebrations, to mark the relief of Mafeking during the Boer War, but luckily the rest was saved by the vicar of the time!

Nearby is the Bywells spring, which many older villagers can remember as their only source of water, which had to be fetched in buckets. The flow had never been known to fail until the drought of 1976.

The 'Manor House', an attractive old building near the back gates of Witham Hall, is a misnomer. It was, in fact, the living quarters for the servants who worked at Witham Hall. The pillared cottage is an attractive stone cottage, believed to have been built about the same time as the Hall. It was originally the gatekeeper's cottage and the wrought iron gates mark the old entrance to the park and Hall, in the times of horse-drawn carriages. The pillars at the 'front' of the cottage were added in the 1960s but the pillars at the side are original. The right-hand side of the cottage used to be a dairy many years ago.

'The Anvils', a modern house near the church, stands on the site of the old blacksmith's forge.

Woodhall Spa 🐾

The village has some 2,500 inhabitants, an abundance of trees and is situated almost at the centre of Lincolnshire.

The road from Lincoln (B1191) crosses the river Witham at Kirkstead Bridge and enters the village along the tree-lined Witham Road. The gravestones and the war memorial at the crossroads mark the site of the first church to be built in the village, St Andrew's (1847-1957).

Over the crossroads and adjacent to the car park in Station Road is the memorial to 617 (Dambuster) Squadron, RAF. The memorial was dedicated in 1987 and is in the form of a breached dam. The squadron was based at the wartime airfield of Woodhall Spa shortly after the epic dams raid in 1943.

The memorial and the car park are on the site of the Royal Hydro Hotel and Winter Gardens, designed and developed by the architect, R. A. Came, at the end of the 19th century. His plan was based on a rectangular shopping mall and a straight tree-lined Broadway. The hotel was destroyed by an enemy parachute mine in 1943. The only part to survive is the present Mall Hotel, the half-timbered upper storey of which was a style much favoured by Came.

The track of the Kirkstead to Horncastle branch railway (1855-1971) followed the line of the present Clarence Road, behind the Mall Hotel, and crossed Station Road to the Woodhall Spa station, which was sited on the wedge containing the police station and opposite to the post office. The track then continued behind the Broadway shops. Part of the disused railway track now forms part of the long distance footpath, the Viking Way, from the Humber Bridge to Oakham in Leicestershire.

The shops, banks and businesses lining Station Road and the Broadway offer a variety of services and are well able to meet the everyday needs of inhabitants and visitors.

The Golf Hotel at the far end of the Broadway also caters for the needs of the inhabitants and visitors. The building, designed by Came in 1892, originally housed the Clevedon House preparatory school.

Adjacent to the hotel is the 6,300 yard, 18 hole golf course laid down by Harry Vardon and J. H. Taylor in 1905. Later, it was upgraded and is now maintained to championship standards.

Between the Golf Hotel and the Broadway shops is part of Iddesleigh Road, which leads to the Cottage Museum. The aim of the museum is to preserve the community history of Woodhall Spa and district. The nucleus of the exhibits is formed by a collection of photographs and memorabilia of the Wield family, who lived in the building from 1887 until the 1960s.

Across the disused railway track, a private road passes Rose Cottage, which was built in 1873 as a small cottage hospital for the poor. Beyond this point lies the historic heart of the spa. The Tea House in the Woods still provides refreshments in most pleasant surroundings. A delightful place to relax and recall that in the original part of the building (1903) the Misses Williams once served afternoon tea, sold gifts including their own embroidery and provided a lending library service.

The now deserted Rheumatism Clinic encloses the site of the first spa well. It was here, in 1821, John Parkinson of Bolingbroke started to sink a coal mine shaft. After some two to three years and various disasters the shaft was abandoned and covered over. Legend says that when the shaft flooded and overflowed, cattle drinking the water were cured of their ailments. Local inhabitants believed the water relieved the symptoms of rheumatism, gout and scurvy. The lord of the manor, Thomas Hotchkin, believed the water to be beneficial for his gout and built the first Pump Room and Bath House and the Victoria Hotel in 1839. Woodhall Spa was born.

In 1922, Captain Allport converted the cricket pavilion into the Pavilion Cinema with a back projection system. The cinema was the 68th cinema to be opened in the country and became known as the 'Kinema in the Woods'. It was patronised by members of the Royal family during their visits to nearby Petwood. Today, the cinema continues to provide regular entertainment for inhabitants and visitors by showing back projected, up to date, films and by live music from the theatre organ.

In its Edwardian heyday, the spa attracted many visitors including Grace Maple, the only child and heiress of Sir John Blundell Maple (of furniture fame). In 1905, she built a country house in her 'petwood' near to the spa baths and set in 40 acres of rhododendron woods and gardens. The house was called Petwood and became the home of the Weigall family when Grace Maple married Captain, later Sir, Archibald Weigall. In 1933 Lady Weigall converted Petwood into an hotel, in an attempt to offset the problems to the spa caused by the loss of the Victoria Hotel by fire in 1920. In 1943, the hotel became the Officers Mess of 617 (Dambusters) Squadron, RAF. Much memorabilia of the squadron is held in the hotel.

The Weigalls also gave the Jubilee Park to the community. The park commemorating the Silver Jubilee of George V, contains a swimming pool, cricket pitch, tennis courts, bowling greens, children's play area and a caravan site.

Along the Tattershall Road/Abbey Lane is the remaining fragment of the Cistercian abbey of Kirkstead (1187). A little distance from the ruins is the chapel of the abbey, now the church of St Leonard. The church is said to be one of the finest examples of 13th century architecture in Lincolnshire.

Some two and a half miles east of the village, along Kirkby Lane, is Ostlers Plantation. It is the remaining part of several hundred acres of oak and Scotch fir trees planted by John Parkinson and later sold to finance the coal mine project. The plantation provides pleasant woodland walks, and remains of the wartime RAF airfield can be seen.

Woolsthorpe by Belvoir 🐑

Woolsthorpe by Belvoir is in Lincolnshire, but only just. The Leicestershire border is only yards away to the west and the Nottinghamshire border is about four miles to the north-west.

A pleasant place to live with open fields and woods all around, this is hunting country. The Belvoir hounds are kept nearby. Visitors come from all over the world looking for Sir Isaac Newton's birthplace, which is at Woolsthorpe by Colsterworth, but once here they enjoy the scenery! It is confusing having two villages with almost the same name within ten miles of each other.

The church of St James was built in 1847 at a cost of £3,500. It stands about one mile from the original church, which was destroyed by the Roundheads during the Civil War when it is said that it was used to stable their horses overnight. On leaving the next morning the soldiers set fire to the straw and the church burned down. There is also a Methodist chapel.

The village has two public houses, a combined post office and grocer's shop and another grocer's shop at the other end of the village. A village hall opened in 1986 which has a small social club and caters for the sports enthusiasts with football and cricket teams. There is also a youth club and WI.

The county primary school is fighting desperately to stay open, a problem shared by many local schools. A new surgery and health centre is being built.

The population is 410. Employment is found for some at local farms, others go into Grantham to work in factories, and some commute to Nottingham, Peterborough and London. How times have changed. In 1892 the population was over 700, work was found at the local iron ore mines or as stewards, etc at Belvoir Castle. Some worked at Woolsthorpe Stables, built in 1887, looking after the many horses kept there for hunting. Up until 1960 there were seven smallholdings in the village and up to 40 cows were brought up from pasture twice a day to be milked.

The week commencing the first Sunday after the 5th of August has always been kept as Feast Week when visits home were made, a procession to church, dancing, a fair and Flower Show were held. Nowadays, only the Flower Show survives, run by the football club, and a children's sports afternoon. On Spring Bank Holiday Monday a street market is held to raise money for the village hall funds.

This is an estate village but since the 1970s some land has been sold and new houses built, including nine bungalows for senior citizens.

During the Second World War, Woolsthorpe Stables housed many soldiers, including the Durham Light Infantry, the Sherwood Foresters and the Royal Pioneer Corps. Two searchlight batteries were also stationed here. In the First World War, of the young men who answered their country's call, 23 did not return, including three brothers. In the Second World War, nine village men were killed in action or died of wounds.

Wragby

Wragby is a pleasant community situated ten miles from Lincoln on the A158 road to Skegness. Settled originally by the Vikings, it is recorded in the Domesday Book of 1086.

The Market Place contains a number of old and interesting buildings. On the west side, concealed by a modern facade, is a hall house with cruck beams. On the east side is the old manor house and the ancient market hall. Also used at one time as a fire station, it has now become shops. On the north side is a row of Regency buildings including the post office and newly refurbished Turnor Arms, an old coaching inn. Other hostelries are the Adam and Eve (notable for its most interesting pub sign!) and the old Red Lion, which has been a private house for many years.

The Turnor family were generous and benevolent squires of the Panton estate, including Wragby, from the late 17th century until the sudden death of the Squire during the First World War, when the estate was broken up and sold.

In 1698 the Turnor family founded the Turnor's Square hospital and chapel for six clergy widows and six other poor widows or widowers. In 1840 the original buildings were pulled down and twelve new houses built. These were subsequently altered to provide ten houses in the 1950s.

In 1836 the church built in 1200 was in a dilapidated state and Christopher Turnor and 38 other residents petitioned the Bishop of Lincoln for its demolition and for the erection of a new church on land given by Christopher Turnor himself. He also gave £2,000 of the £3,500 which the building cost. The new church in modern Gothic style was consecrated on 4th April 1839. Six bells from the old church were hung in the new belfry. Three of these were cast in Nottingham in 1697 and the other three from the same foundry were brought from Kirmond-le-Mire.

Adjacent to the site of the old church and burial ground is the Routland (tournament place). Ancient earthworks mark the place where Countess Judith, niece of William the Conqueror and resident in Wragby, may well have lived in a manor house surrounded by a timber stockade.

Opposite the vicarage, built in 1811, on the corner of Church Street and Louth Road is the old grammar school, founded by William

Hansard in 1627 and rebuilt in 1775. It is now a listed building and home of Wragby's Amateur Dramatic Society. Also on Louth Road, almost opposite the end of Silver Street, is a house presently used as a private house and office. This is the old parish house, sometimes known as a workhouse or home for the destitute of the parish.

The mill in Bardney Road, built in 1831, lost its sails some years later during a storm.

Wragby like many other places has lost its railway, courthouse and police station (now a private house) and market. Charles II granted a charter for one market and two fairs at the request of the squire, the Duke of Buckingham, and eggs and butter were still sold at the market in the early part of the 20th century. The cattle market continued until after the Second World War.

However, Wragby is still a flourishing community with a modern Town Hall, built in the 1950s and well used by many organisations.

About 100 council houses and a similar number of private homes have been built since the 1960s and more are planned. There is some light industry offering employment to local people. This includes a timber yard, a plastics factory making items for the medical world and the manufacture of beehives and bee-keeping equipment.

Wrangle

Wrangle is situated off the A52, only a short distance from the shores of the Wash. It was spelled Weranghe in the Domesday Book, and in the 15th century, Wranghill.

The church of St Mary and St Nicholas is built in the late Norman and Early English style with later additions. It has a fine pulpit of the Elizabethan period and a tower with six bells.

Wrangle was quite an important village in the 13th and 14th centuries, with a thriving market which served the surrounding area. This was held on Saturdays. In 1359 when Edward III was raising a navy to invade France, this village was one of 82 places in the kingdom asked to send help. Wrangle sent one ship and eight men, more than Liverpool who only sent one ship and five men.

The bedehouse and school were founded in 1555 by Thomas Alenson. He gave his house at Joy Hill to be converted into a bedehouse for three poor men and two poor women, one of whom should be able to instruct the children in English and Latin. In 1705 Rev William

Erskine gave nine acres of land, the rent from which was used to make up the weekly salaries and stipends of the five members of the bede-house, and also to pay the schoolmaster.

The chief crops grown in the area in 1889 were corn, potatoes, man-gel-wurzels and turnips, with a lot of rich pasture land. Today farming is still a very important industry in the village, with some of the best quality land in the county.

A piece of land in the parish is called Kings Hill, which at one time was moated and evidently was the site of a house of some importance. It is near Wrangle Common. Another place also moated round was called Ivory. Extensive foundations have been found in both places. Ivory is on the Friskney parish border.

On the ploughing up of Wrangle Common a great number of balls of burnt clay were found. These were moulded in the hand by compressing the fingers, the impressions of which were still visible, but the purpose of these is not clear.

Many human bones were dug up in a part of the village called Gallows Marsh. In 1852 an ancient brass ring, once thickly gilded, was found in the vicarage garden, engraved 'en bon an'. It is thought to have been a New Year gift, dating from the late 15th century.

Joseph Gilbert, a member of an old Wrangle family, was attached to the first expedition under Captain Cook, and gave his name to the locality in the Pacific called Gilbert's Island.

In 1977, the year of the Queen's Silver Jubilee, the annual Flower Show was revived. It had lapsed for several years, owing to bad weath-er, but is now held on the first Saturday in July. It used to be held on a Thursday and goes back over 100 years.

Wyham cum Cadeby

This joint parish, lying on the west side of Barton Street, is all that remains of two religious houses, plus their attendant workers' cottages.

Wyham is thought to be a place of great antiquity, as the name means in Old English 'a heathen temple'. There was a monastery here in medieval times, with its fish ponds and farm buildings, but today the area is a farming estate.

Wyham House, parts of which date from the 14th century, is a fine building and stands opposite All Saints' church, now disused, which was rebuilt in 1886 on the site of a much earlier building. The rectory is was rebuilt in 1886 on the site of a much earlier building. The rectory is much restored and is lived in, and there are some farm workers' houses.

North-west of Wyham stands Cadeby, called Catebi in the Domesday Book. There was a nunnery here in the Middle Ages, and there are extensive ruins underground. Cadeby Hall is no longer occupied and is boarded up. The adjoining land is farmed, and game birds are reared. There are some cottages and farm buildings. It is said that underground passages link Cadeby and Wyham.

188

Index